"Innovative and thoughtful, *P is for Pleasanton* is a fun, kid-f
stories to life and celebrates what makes Pleasanton specia

ALAMEDA COUNTY FAIR

MW01681631

"*P is for Pleasanton* perfectly captures the charm, character, and small-town feel that so many of us love about this community. From its rich history to its beloved local landmarks, this book is a wonderful reminder of what makes Pleasanton such a special place to call home."

GABRIELLE WELK | EXECUTIVE DIRECTOR, PLEASANTON DOWNTOWN ASSOCIATION

"*P is for Pleasanton* captures the heart of our community in a way that children and families will love. Kori and Sammy bring Pleasanton to life through local pride, familiar places, and the simple joy of learning about the place we call home."

TONY CRUZ | EXECUTIVE DIRECTOR, MUSEUM ON MAIN

"*P is for Pleasanton* is a beautiful celebration of this community's past, present and future. The vibrant artwork and engaging stories reflect the heart of Pleasanton that has been beating with passion and pride for more than 150 years."

JEREMY WALSH | ASSOCIATE PUBLISHER, *PLEASANTON WEEKLY*

"Kori and Sammy have created an entertaining and accurate history of Pleasanton including the challenging X, Y, and Z! Well done! Every resident and visitor to Pleasanton needs this book."

JUDY WHEELER | OWNER, TOWNE CENTER BOOKS

"This unique book has paintings and vignettes which provide readers with a new look at Pleasanton. For young and old alike, *P is for Pleasanton* is a must read."

BEVERLY LANE | LOCAL HISTORIAN, AUTHOR *DANVILLE, HEART OF THE SAN RAMON VALLEY*

Visit us online | **WWW.HOMETOWNALPHABET.COM**

Instagram @HometownHighlightsAlphabet | **Facebook** Hometown Highlights Alphabet Series

Note From the Authors

Friends,

It is simply not possible to squeeze a city's fullness into a few dozen pages and just as many paintings. The unique places, people, and compelling stories that make Pleasanton special are countless! So, here we are, merely scratching the surface with 26 highlights of the city's past (from the mid-1800s) and present, in a way that kids and families can enjoy together. While many treasured destinations, history, and anecdotes could not be included, we hope that the sites and activities mentioned in the following pages (and challenge check-list in the back!) kindle your desire to dig deeper into local history and inspire thankfulness for the beautiful place you call home.

The books in our Hometown Highlights Alphabet series - ***C is for Concord, W is for Walnut Creek, C is for Clayton, B is for Brentwood, M is for Martinez, L is for Livermore***, and those still to come - overflow from our thankful hearts for the beautiful San Francisco Bay Area where God has placed us. What began as a fun, simple, local history project to give to our children grew into a gift of love for our community at large. We delight in words, old books (they're good friends of ours), language, and art, and we strive to use our gifts to glorify God and bless our community through this book series (1 Corinthians 10:31).

There are many terrific aspects that we love about writing and illustrating books, but we are particularly thankful for the connections with locals that we have made, and continue to make, on this journey. It makes us smile! And we hope that the paintings, poems, and history within these pages make *you* smile, too, and encourage you to learn more about your hometown.

Remember: everything has a story.

Happy reading!

Kori & Sammy Barton

Husband-and-Wife Author/Illustrator Duo

ISBN 979-8-9895542-6-3

The illustrations for this book are rendered in acrylic paint and ink.

Mustard Palace BOOKS

AN A-Z JOURNEY THROUGH PLEASANTON, CALIFORNIA

P IS FOR PLEASANTON

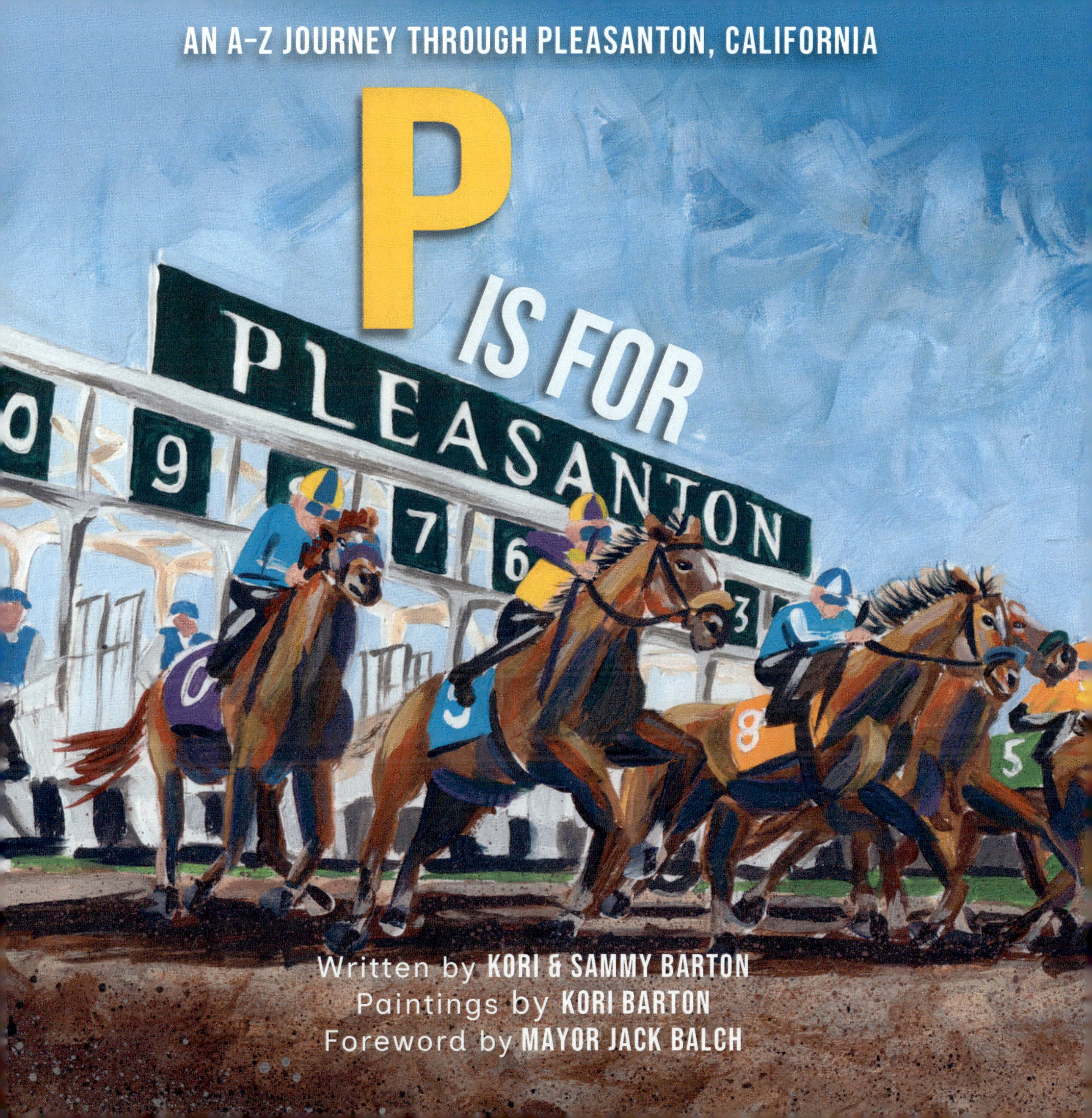

Written by KORI & SAMMY BARTON

Paintings by KORI BARTON

Foreword by MAYOR JACK BALCH

Foreword

Dear Readers,

Welcome to *P is for Pleasanton*! This is a journey through the city so many of us are proud to call home. Sitting among rolling hills and oak-studded landscapes, Pleasanton is a place where history, community, and opportunity come together in special ways. From our vibrant downtown and beautiful parks to our schools, traditions, and local landmarks, every letter in this book tells a piece of the story that makes Pleasanton unique.

One of the things I love most about Pleasanton is that it is a community built by people who care deeply about one another. Whether it's neighbors gathering for a parade, families enjoying a summer concert, volunteers giving their time, or students dreaming about what they can become, Pleasanton shines because of the people who call it home. This book beautifully captures the places, experiences, and values that connect us.

As you explore these pages, I hope you'll discover something new about Pleasanton. Most importantly, I hope this book inspires young readers to be curious, engaged, and proud of their hometown. Enjoy the adventure of reading!

Warmly,

Jack Balch
Mayor, City of Pleasanton
June 2026

Dedicated to every kid in Pleasanton:
May you always give thanks for the beautiful city you call home!

And to Aunt Dubes: Your enthusiasm for Pleasanton's history is infectious!
Thanks for getting us started on this book.

♡ K.B. & S.B.
Soli Deo Gloria!

Contents

Honorable Mentions

How difficult it is to narrow Pleasanton's history down to 26 highlights!
Here are a few additional gems of the city's past:

JOHNSTON BUILDING (1896)
GAY 90'S PIZZERIA (C.1864)
NEW LINCOLN THEATRE/ROXY THEATER (1927)
HERITAGE HOUSE (C.1900)
THE PLEASANTON HOTEL (1864)
BERNAL ADOBE BUILDING (1850)

A stands for ALVISO, who helped manage ranches,
and built his own house using mud, straw and branches.
You might not want to live in a mud house, that's fine,
but it's lasted way longer than your house or mine!

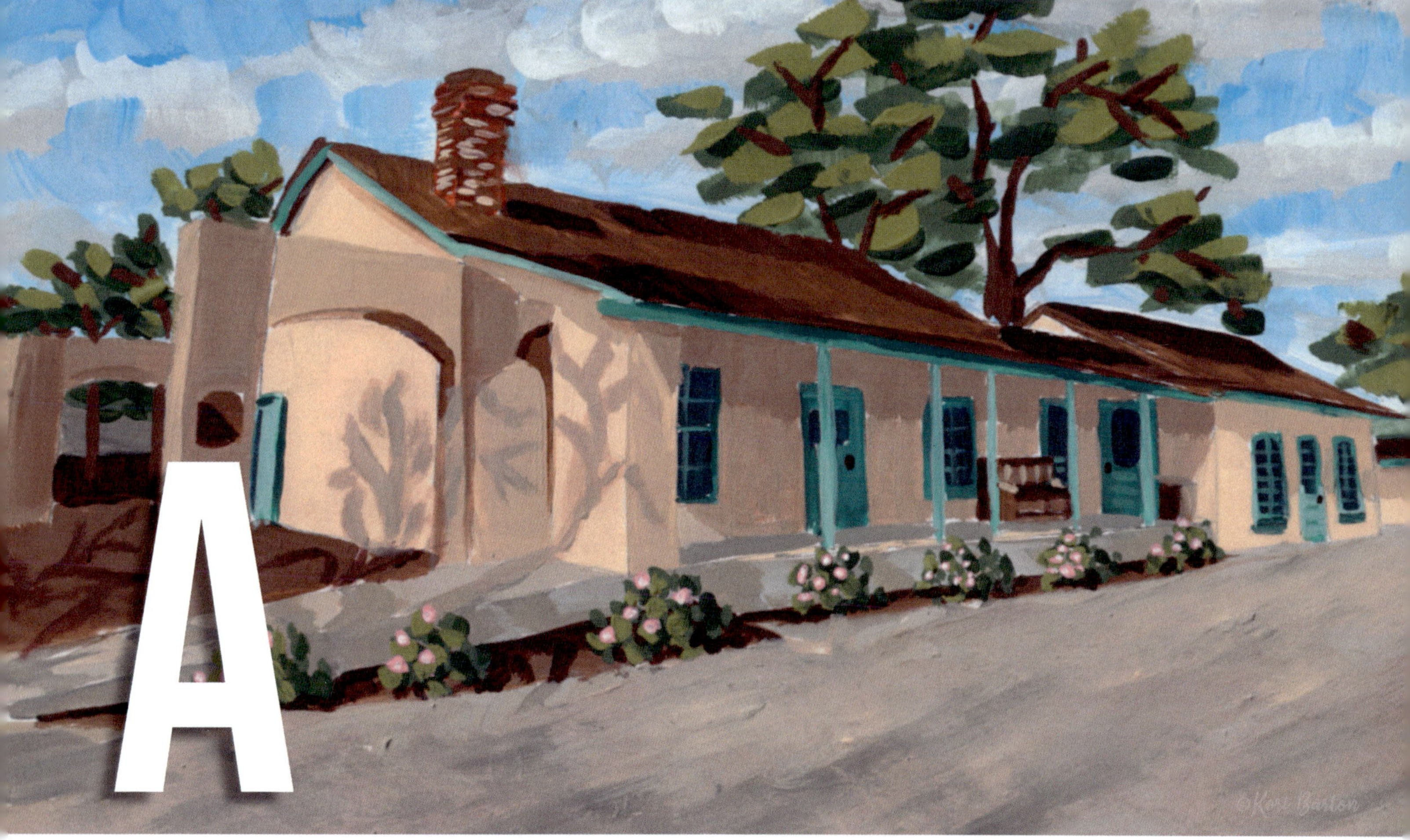

A

Francisco Alviso was a respectable ***moyordomo***, or ranch foreman, for many local ranch owners in the mid 1800s during the Spanish and Mexican land grant period. The local ranch owners included Mr. Sunol, Mr. Pacheco, Mr. Amador, and the Bernals. Father of 19 children, Alviso built an adobe (pictured) for his family in 1854. It was the first adobe built in the Pleasanton Valley. The home had dirt floors and burlap ceilings until the early 1900s. At various times, the home was surrounded by cattle, horses, and golden fields of grain and sugar beet crops. This adobe was so well-built and carefully maintained that it was continuously in use for 115 years! It is one of the oldest surviving buildings in Pleasanton and shares space at the Alviso Adobe Community Park with the old Meadowlark Dairy milking barn and the bunkhouse on Old Foothill Road. The Adobe has been fully restored and stands to tell the story of California's history to visitors of all ages.

To some it just looks like big piles of dirt,
to others, a place they would likely get hurt.
But for kids who like riding, they can fly and be free,
at the BMX Park which begins with a B.

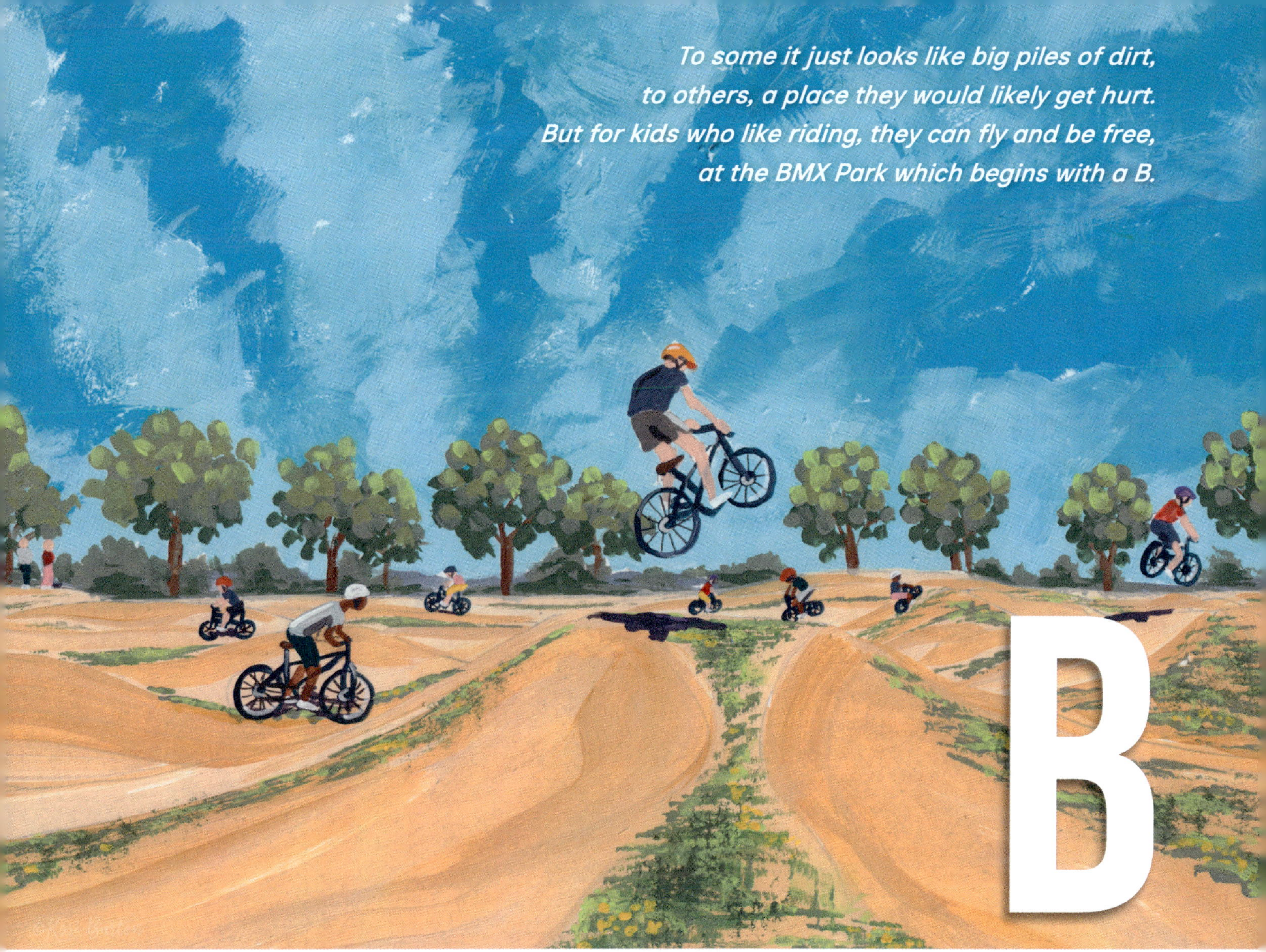

B

Inspired by the sport of motocross, BMX riding became hugely popular in Southern California during the 1960s and quickly gained momentum. BMX courses made their way up to Northern California in the 1970s. In the summer of 2005, the City of Pleasanton opened the 3.65 acre BMX Park on Stanley Boulevard. With dirt mounds and berms aplenty, this course provides a great way for biking enthusiasts of all ages and skill levels to try new things and enjoy being outside. There are tracks designed for beginners and more complex tracks for experienced riders. For beginner riders, it might be intimidating, but after your first run, you're bound to go back for more. And since admission is free, and it's open sunrise to sunset year-round (except for weather-related closures during the winter months), there is no reason not to give it a try!

Letter C stands for CANDY CANE LANE with its lights
that twinkle and glow on crisp December nights.
Other folks deck the halls, but THEY deck the whole street,
for seventy-years it's been a holiday treat!

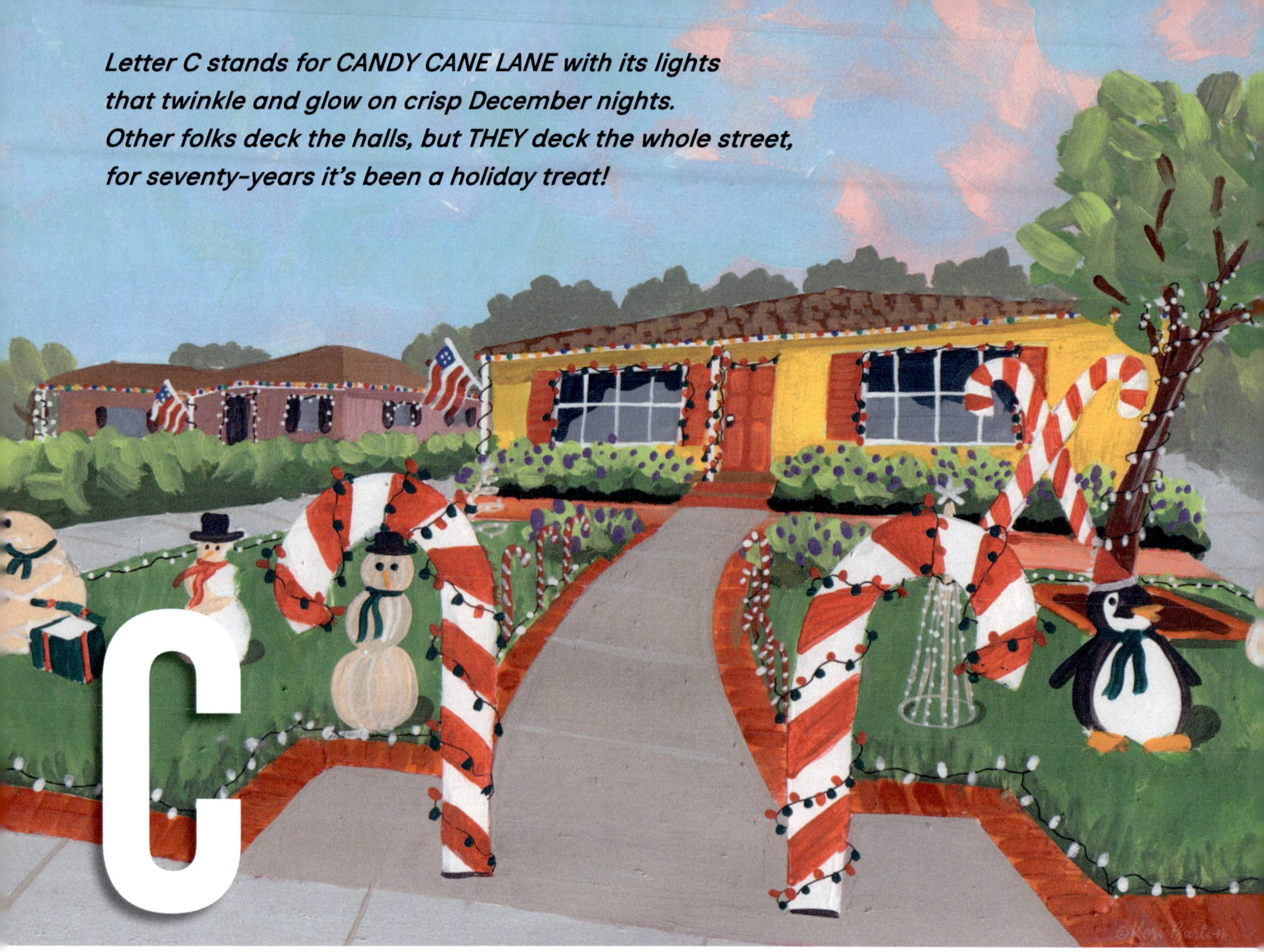

C

Every December since 1955, Candy Cane Lane in Pleasanton, known during the rest of the year as Walnut Drive, heralds one of the most impressive and long-lived Christmas light displays in the Bay Area. Each house and yard is uniquely decorated, and some of the original owners or their children are still living there, faithfully carrying on the tradition. "All 28 homes [on the street] turn on their displays at the exact same time, right after the downtown parade," says Candy Cane Lane neighbor Robin Cruz. "The street suddenly transforms from darkness to full blown decorations and stays lit for the entire month!" And it all started with Milton and Juanita Regalia in 1953 when they decorated their yard with Milton's beautiful hand-painted decorations. When you visit, keep an eye out for the original wooden candy cane decorations which have been the street's mascot for 71 years and counting!

The D in this town stands for Meadowlark DAIRY,
with flavors of soft serve like orange and berry.
They used to sell milk from their farm with livestock,
and now lines for ice cream stretch clear 'round the block!

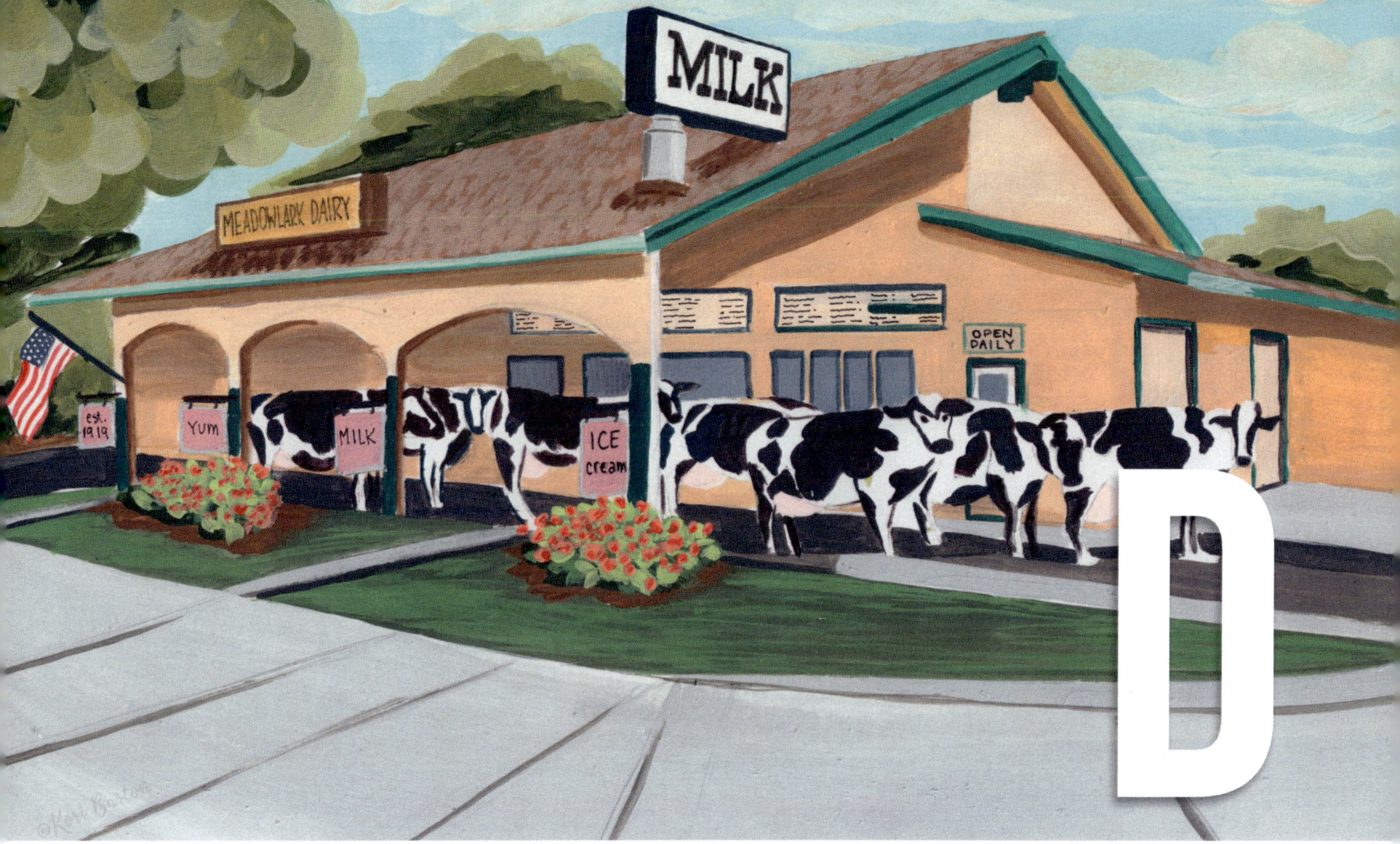

D

The beloved Meadowlark Dairy began when Walter M. Briggs bought the Alviso Adobe property in 1919 (see letter A). More than 150 acres on Old Foothill Road was home to the Meadowlark Dairy from 1923 until they relocated the retail shop to their current location on West Neal Street in 1969. During Meadowlark's busy seasons, they see about 170,000 people every month and sell a whopping 1,400 gallons of ice cream every week! "For our family it has been a wild ride," says owner Jesse Takens. "My grandparents immigrated here with $20 in their pocket in the 1950s and ended up managing and later buying the dairy in the 1960s and moved it downtown. Then my parents really turned it into a special place in the community. They're the ones who put in the hard work. For my wife, our kids, and myself it's been an honor to be involved. We love being immersed in our community!"

E stands for ESTATE of the kind Phoebe Hearst
who had enough money to make a bank burst.
But she was a wise and generous giver
and the causes she helped to prosper outlive her.

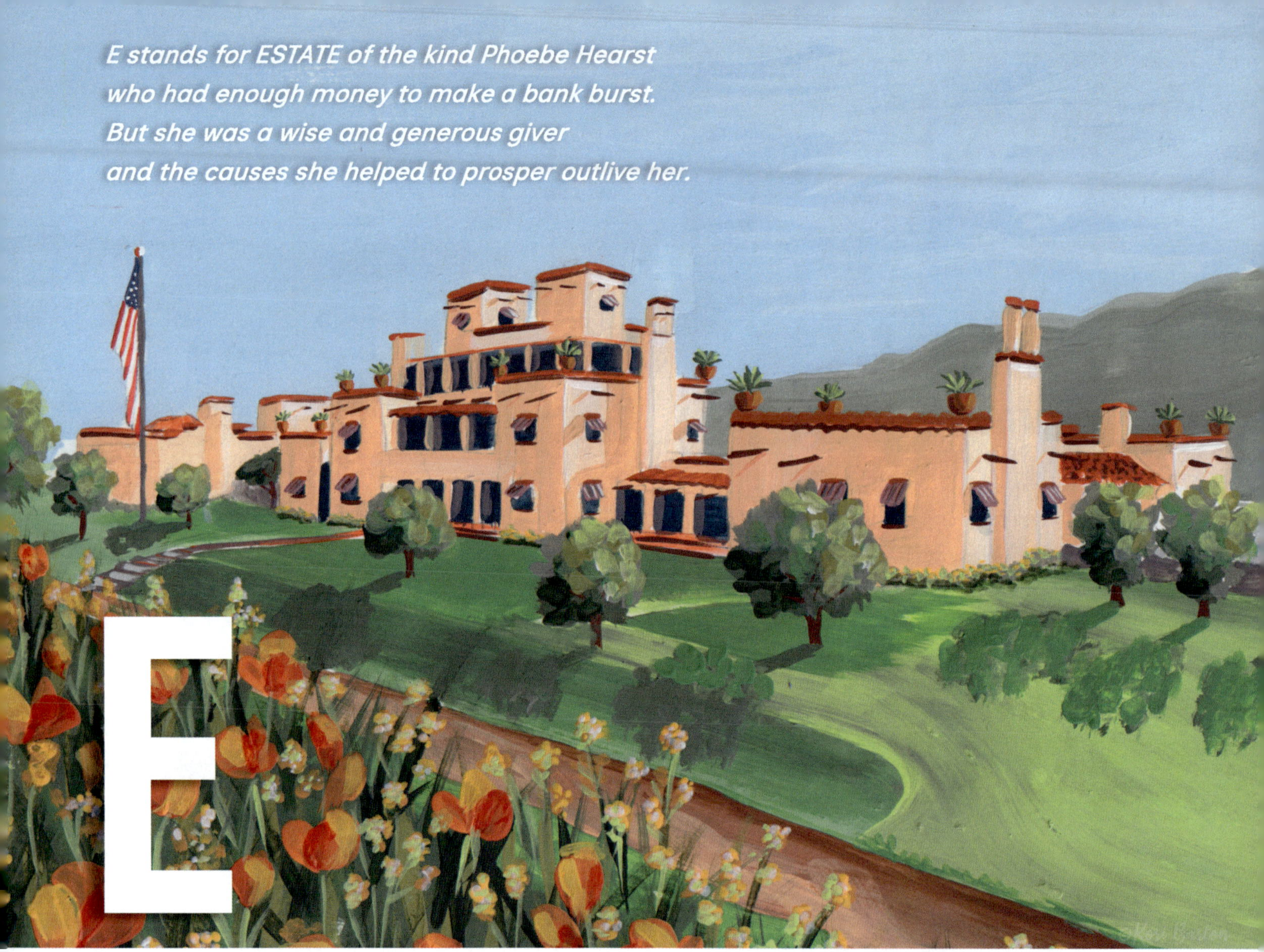

Mrs. Phoebe Hearst, a school teacher from Missouri, built the sprawling 53-room "Hacienda del Pozo de Verona" (Estate of the Verona Well, pictured) on a hill in south Pleasanton in 1899 after she inherited her husband George Hearst's estate. George was an exceedingly wealthy gold, silver, and copper miner and owned more than one-million acres of land. After George died, Phoebe learned how to manage his business. She become an excellent businesswoman and an extraordinarily generous giver. It was her joy to care for all people (presidents and poor folk alike), host parties, and financially support educational causes, including libraries and schools across the country. When she died on April 13, 1919, flags were flown at half mast to honor her life. Sadly, the beautiful Hacienda burned down in 1969, but the humble and generous legacy of Phoebe lives on. The Sausalito News put it best on April 19, 1919: "Mrs. Hearst crowded more of kindness and beneficence to American men, women, and children than has been accomplished by any other woman of her time."

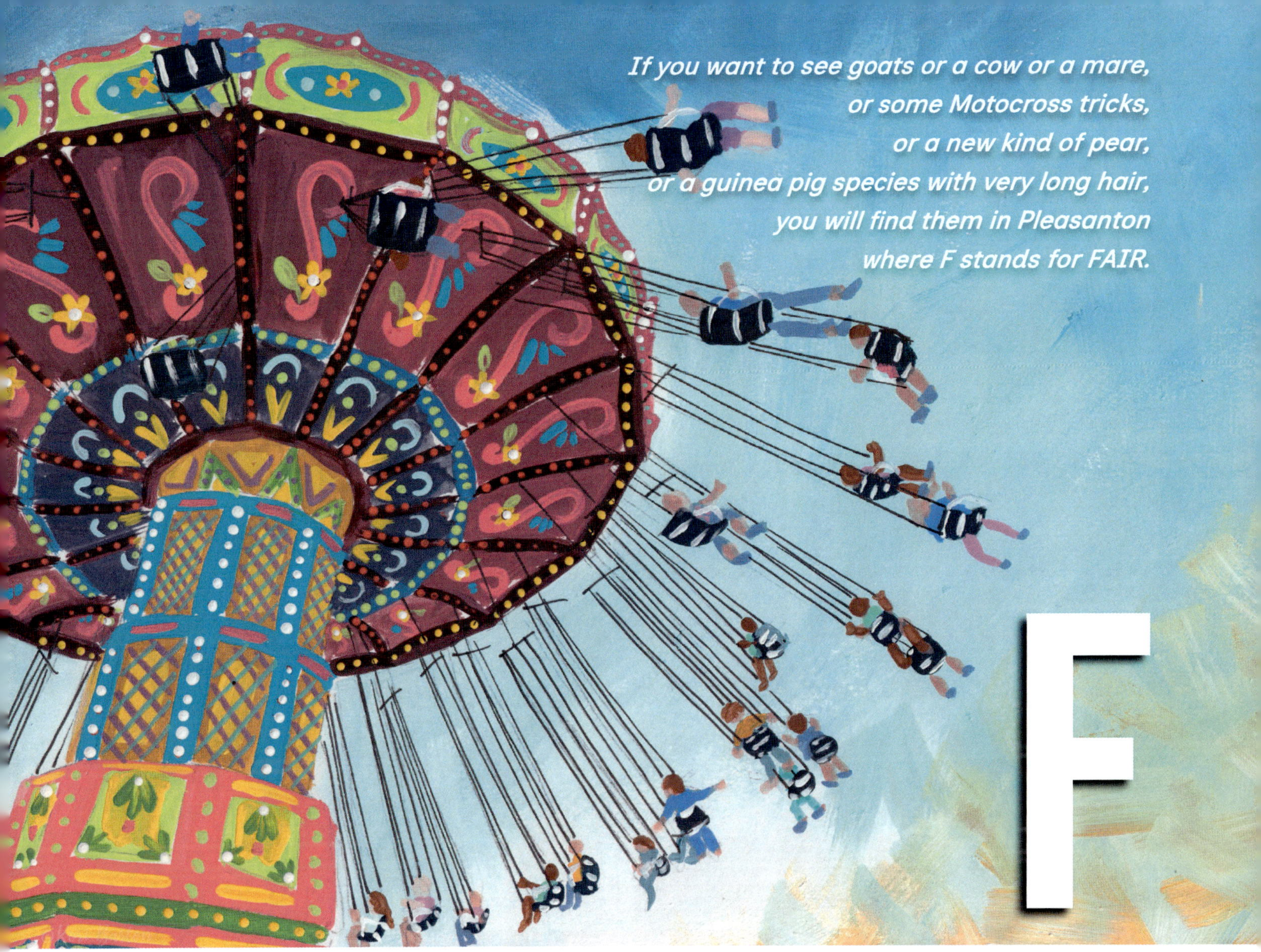

If you want to see goats or a cow or a mare,
or some Motocross tricks,
or a new kind of pear,
or a guinea pig species with very long hair,
you will find them in Pleasanton
where F stands for FAIR.

F

The Bernal family built a one-mile horse racetrack in 1858 (see letter J), and the first Alameda County Fair was held on the site in October 1912. And how it has grown! In recent years, more than 400,000 annual attendees have enjoyed racing pigs, BMX shows, hot air balloon rides, concerts, 4-H animal auctions, and many exhibits. But its roots are firmly planted in agriculture. The fair originally was held in the fall and centered mainly around horse racing, along with farming machines, a variety of local crops, homemade goods, and handicrafts. Nowadays, a favorite for kids is strolling through the art exhibits and the small animal exhibits where breeds of rabbits, guinea pigs, turkeys, and more are on display. Though much has changed at the annual fair during the last century, it maintains Pleasanton's legacy of local farming and agriculture through exhibits and displays like the American Farm Tractor Museum.

G stands for GRAVEYARD to honor those passed,
their names carved in stone so their memory can last.
Here founders and heroes and pioneers lay,
their important legacies shall not fade away.

G

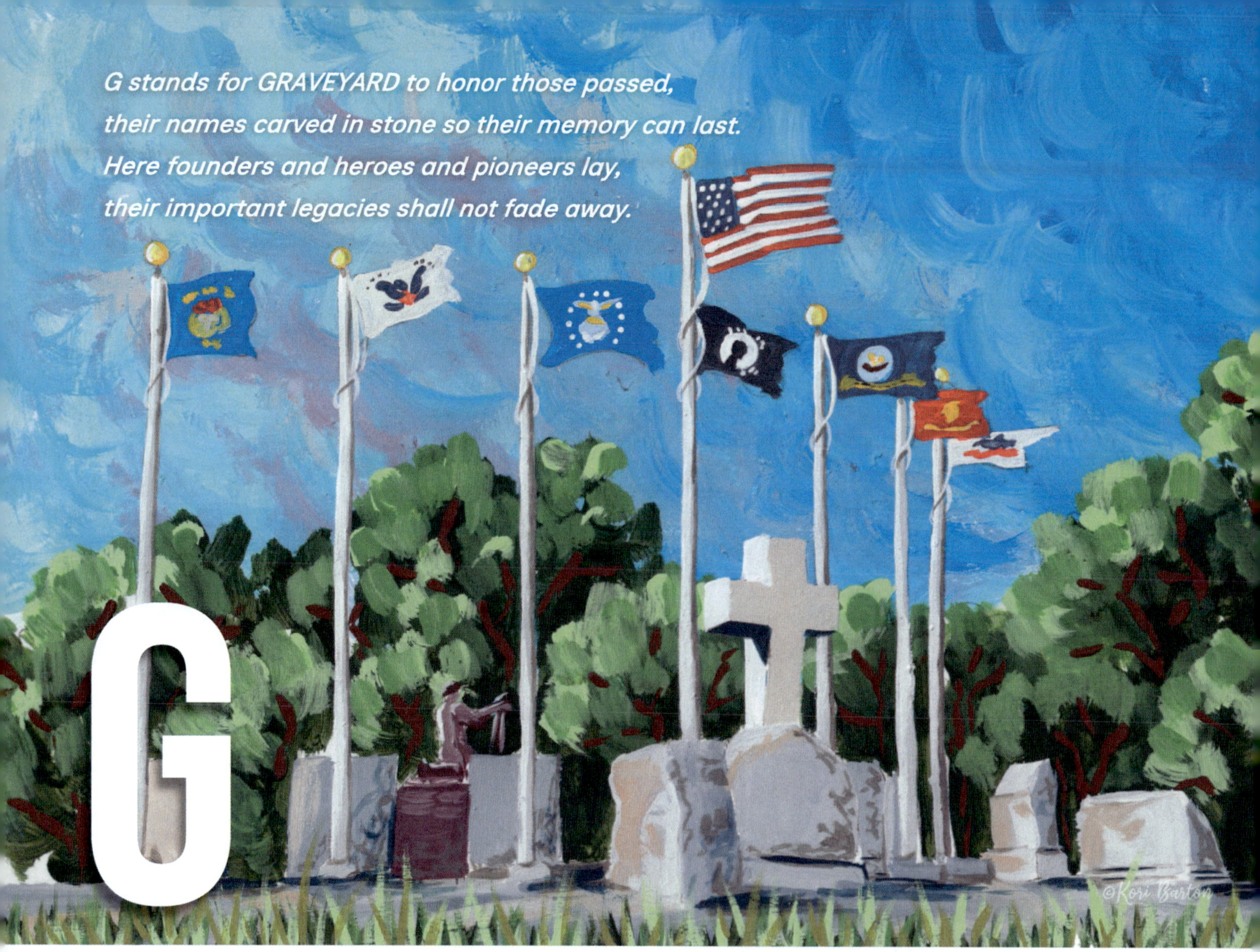

High up on a hill in the southern end of Pleasanton, through an old, iron gate, sits Pleasanton Memorial Gardens, the first cemetery in Pleasanton. The Independent Order of Odd Fellows (IOOF) established this graveyard in 1886 and maintained it for the next 120 years. The City of Pleasanton has owned the property since 2007 and renamed it the Pleasanton Pioneer Cemetery. If you walk along the grassy hillside, you'll find memorial stones for many of the city's pioneers including Joshua Ayers Neal, John Kottinger, the Bernal family, along with a number of military veterans from Pleasanton. A beautiful Veterans Memorial was established in the cemetery in 2016 (pictured) honoring all U.S. military Veterans and dedicated specifically to Veterans of Pleasanton. In May, the American Legion honors military grave sites with military medallions and American flags placed on the memorial stones of every veteran, and does the same with wreaths in December.

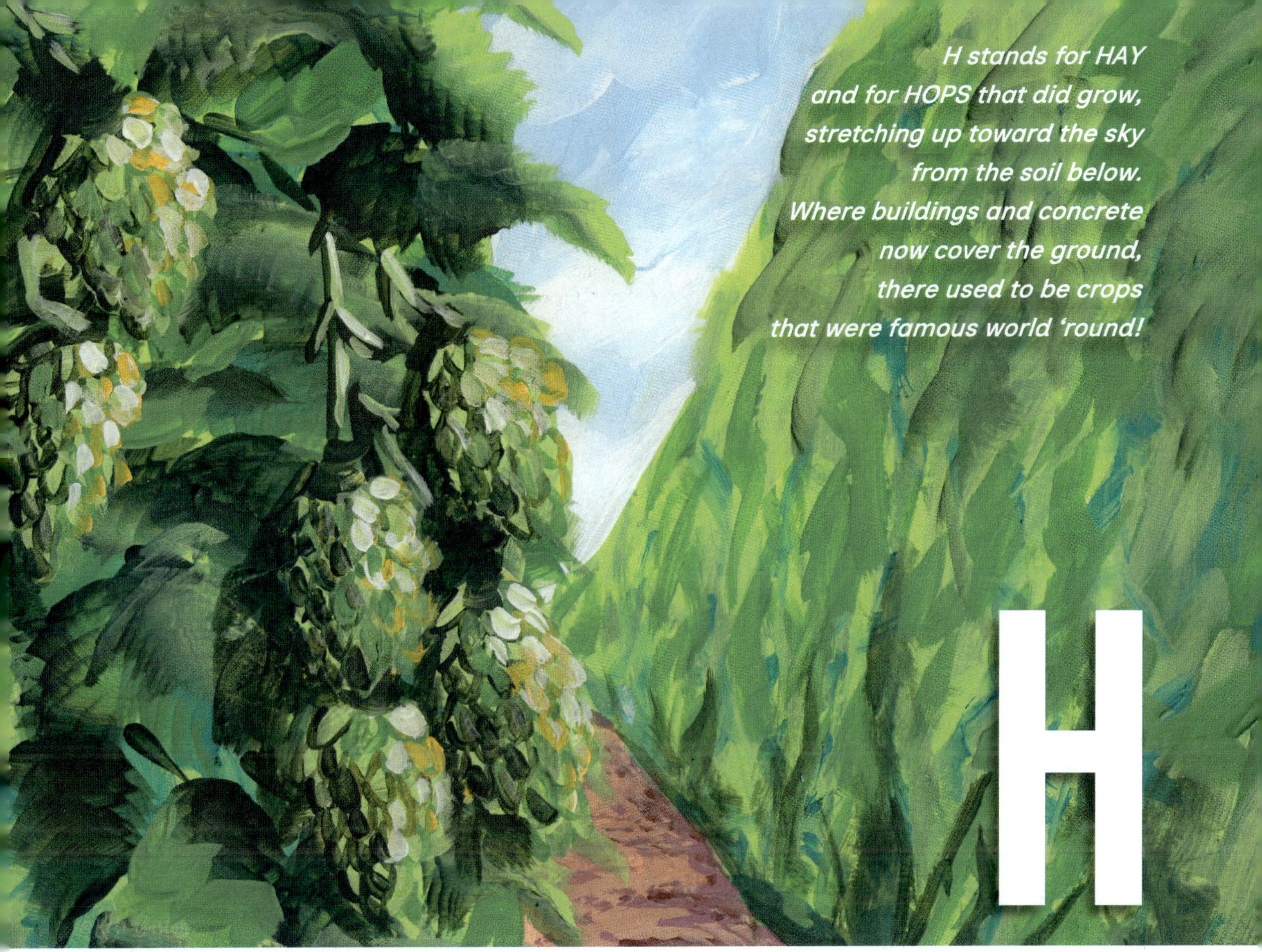

H stands for HAY
and for HOPS that did grow,
stretching up toward the sky
from the soil below.
Where buildings and concrete
now cover the ground,
there used to be crops
that were famous world 'round!

H

Many streets in town are named after important local people and commodities from the 19th-20th centuries, Hopyard Road being one of them. In the 1880s, hops fields were planted and the shipping of harvested hops nationally and internationally became a significant source of income for Pleasanton. By 1900, Pleasanton was the largest hops growing area in the state. Hops fields lined each side of the aptly named road for more than a mile. The temperate climate and historically soggy soil enabled the plants to grow along towering 20-foot tall trellises. Come September, the flowering crops were harvested by hand, dried in massive kilns, and shipped to beer manufacturers around the world. Sugar beets, "Pleasanton Hay" (famous among horse breeders as far as England!). Other grain crops were also prolific in the area through the mid-1900s. Many homes in modern-day Pleasanton rest on former farmlands. What crop do you think was once grown in your yard?

In the mid 1800's the roads were so bumpy,
the bouncing could make even cheerful folks grumpy.
'Til a Pleasanton man made a brand new suspension,
and to honor his efforts, "I" stands for INVENTION.

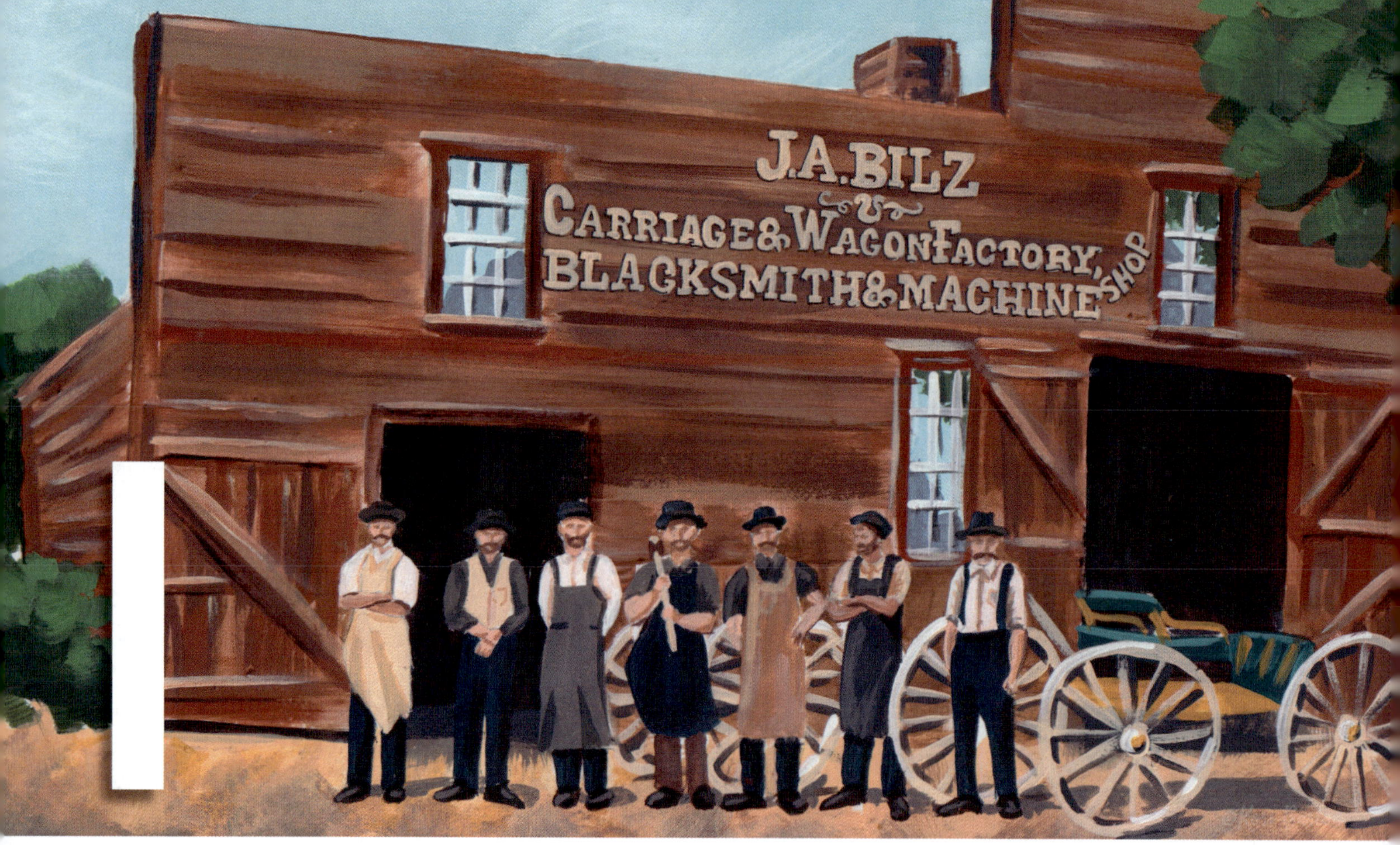

The pioneers of the 1800s knew how to work hard and take initiative. When not busy in the field, many folks put their hands and minds toward inventing new machinery. One such man was John A. Bilz of Pleasanton who patented three machines between 1882-1892. A skilled blacksmith, Bilz built the J. A. Bilz Carriage and Wagon Factory in 1865 at the corner of Main Street and Spring Street where he perfected his two-wheeled wagon and a gang-plow. His "Bilz Excelsior" two-wheeled vehicle patented in 1882 made travel by horse "easy and pleasant" for riders traveling over rough roads. He perfected the buggy seat in 1886, making a lighter "speeding-cart" that sat more closely to the horse. His final invention in 1892 was a plow built specifically for use in narrow spaces where, "the plowing must be done close to the trees yet not injure them." He saw problems and created solutions. Three cheers for the innovative pioneers!

Some cities love soccer, some cities love hockey,
but there's racing in Pleasanton, so the J stand for JOCKEY.
You can watch horses load in and burst from the gates,
at the oldest racetrack in the whole 50 states!

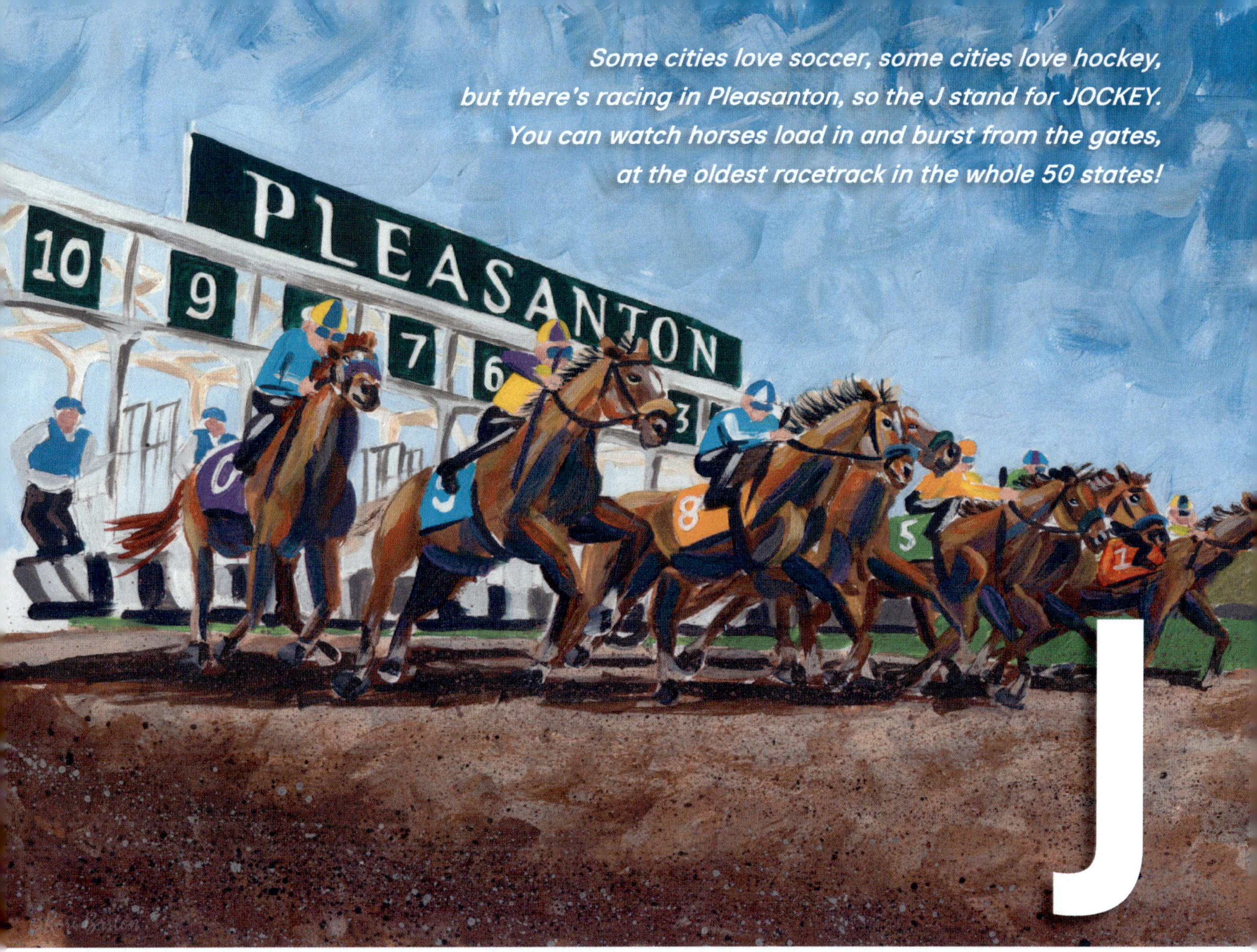

J

Pleasanton is home to the oldest one-mile horse racetrack in the United States! Built in the 1850s by local Mexican land grant owner Augustin Bernal, the Pleasanton track, along with a world-class horse training and breeding facility, became famous around the globe. Pleasanton's mild climate, ideal clay soil composition which cushioned the horses hooves, and Mr. Bernal's excellent horsemanship were the ingredients that helped shape the legacy of horse racing in the city. Even Seabiscuit, the legendary racehorse, trained and raced at this facility in the 1930s. The horses were originally raced with their drivers in a buggy (see letter "I"), and later jockeys sat in the "jockey crouch" atop the horses backs. Buggy, or harness racing, ended in 1968. The track's history following its opening is peppered with numerous successes as well as defeats, including a 16-year racing closure between 1916-1932. The racetrack closed again in March 2025, but locals remain hopeful that racing will return to Pleasanton someday soon.

John KOTTINGER starts with a K, that's a fact,
and he's one local man who made quite an impact.
He founded the city, had talents galore;
you can go see his barn if you want to learn more.

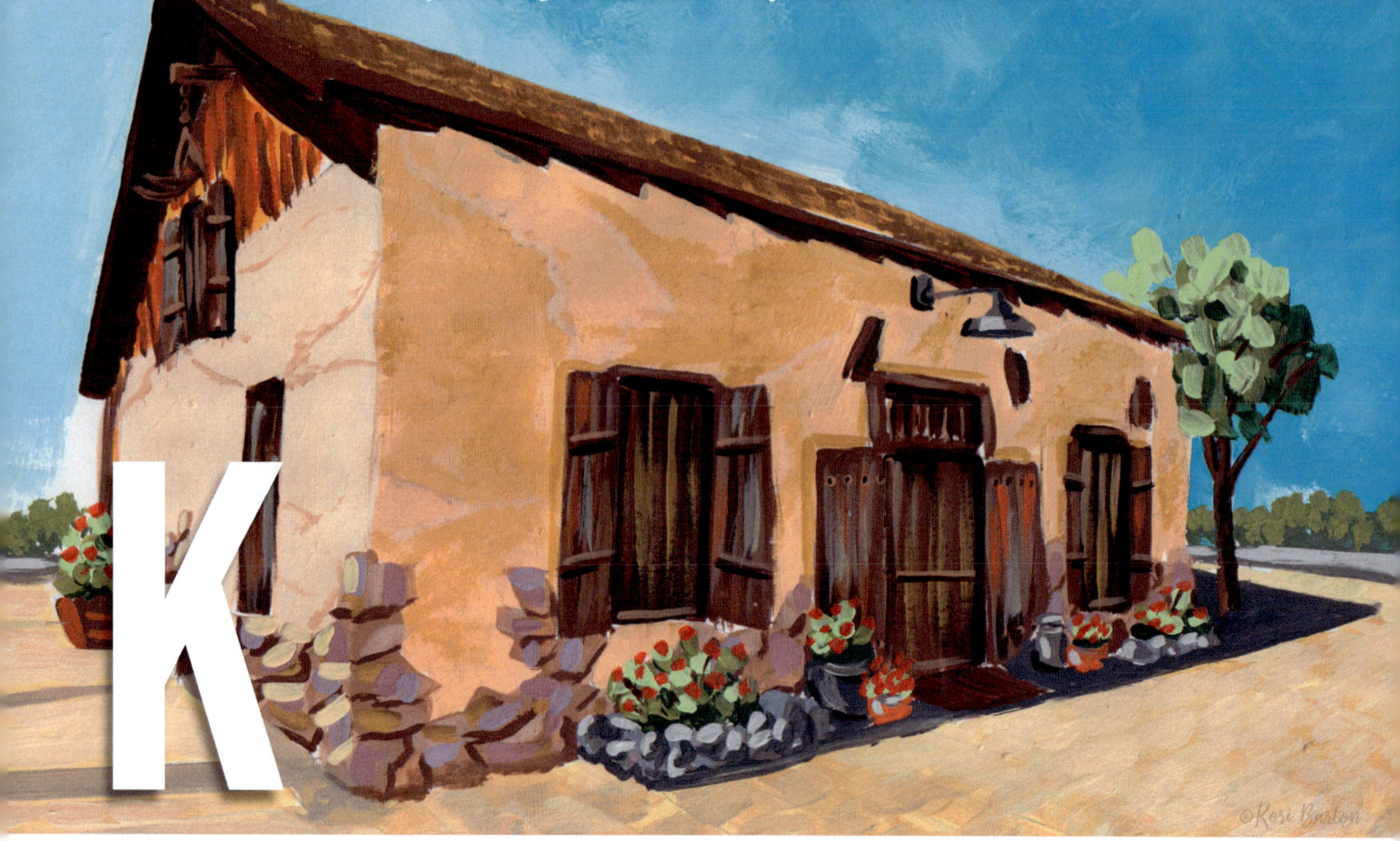

John William Kottinger (1819-1892), known as "The Father of Pleasanton," was a name that all locals would have recognized and respected in the mid 1800s. This leading citizen and true jack-of-all-trades came from Austria in 1849. He was a savvy businessman, builder, teacher, store owner, notary, cattleman, vineyardist, lawyer, translator, and founder of Pleasanton. He married a daughter of well-known Juan Pablo Bernal, who owned a large Mexican land grant including the area of what is now Pleasanton. Kottinger built the adobe barn (pictured) in 1851 on Ray Street. The legend goes that this adobe was used a jail when Kottinger was elected as the first Justice of the Peace in the Murray Township, part of Alameda County encompassing Pleasanton. It is one of only a few adobe barns remaining in California. The barn was carefully restored in 1984 and again in recent years, and it retains the original hay hoist and metal bars on the windows.

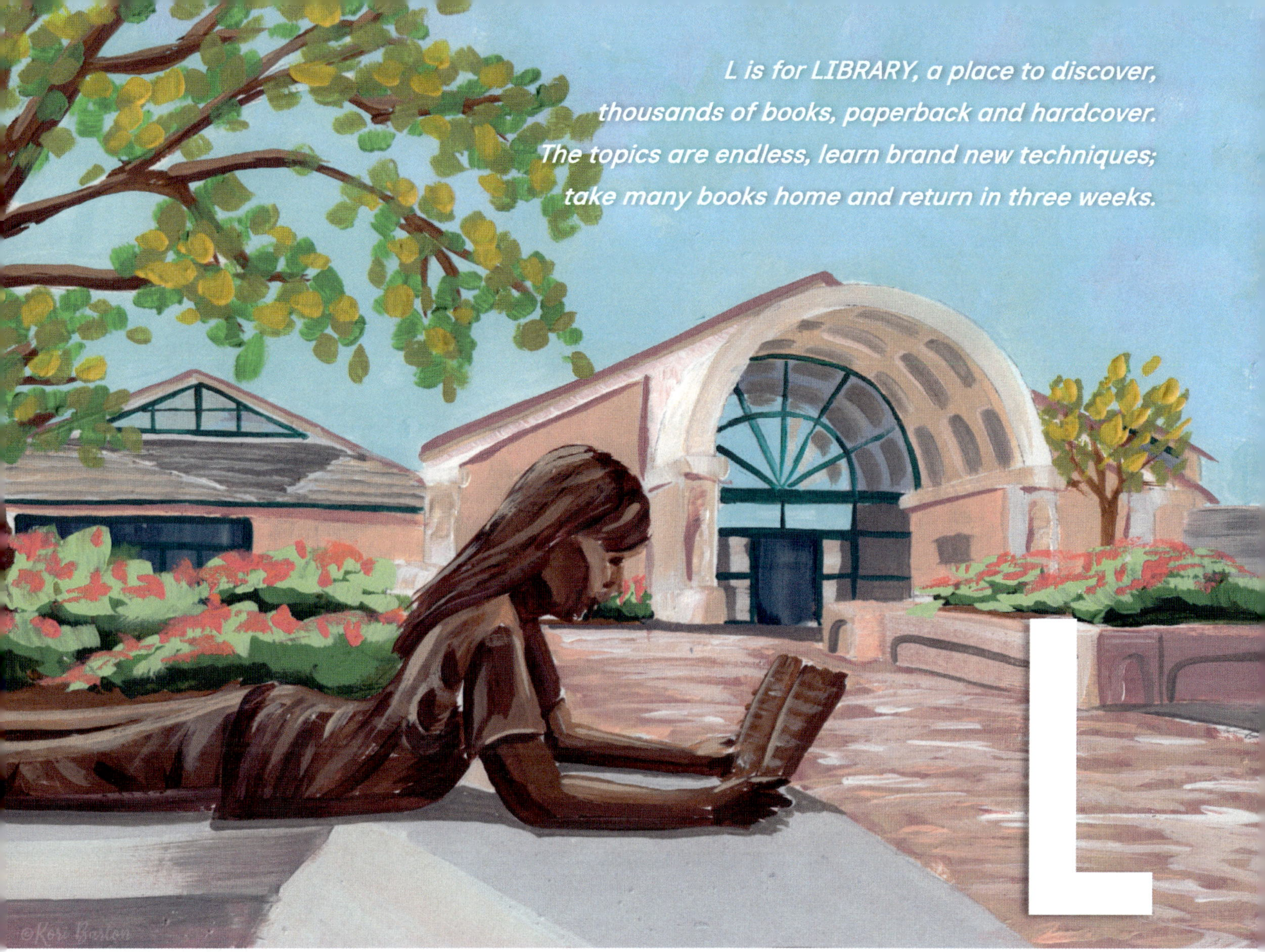

L is for LIBRARY, a place to discover,
thousands of books, paperback and hardcover.
The topics are endless, learn brand new techniques;
take many books home and return in three weeks.

L

Various locations in Pleasanton have housed libraries over the past century, and it is all thanks to the Women's Improvement Club. In 1909, the club raised money to acquire land at Main Street and Division Street (modern day Museum on Main; see letter M) and proudly opened the first reading room. Since then, the library has occupied temporary buildings, small buildings, and even no building at all between 1967-68 while a new location was identified. Today's enormous and welcoming library, opened in 1988 on Old Bernal Avenue, is home to more than 170,000 items in its collection. This library hosts special events, story time, clubs, meetings, tutoring, adult education, and more. In recent years, more than 800,000 items have been borrowed annually! The Pleasanton library is a treasured hub for the community, and you can access it all with your very own library card. Next time you visit the library, remember that it began as just a simple, small reading room.

It's important to learn how things were long ago,
we can see where we came from and where we might go.
So, to help you keep facts from the past in your brain,
the letter M stands for MUSEUM ON MAIN.

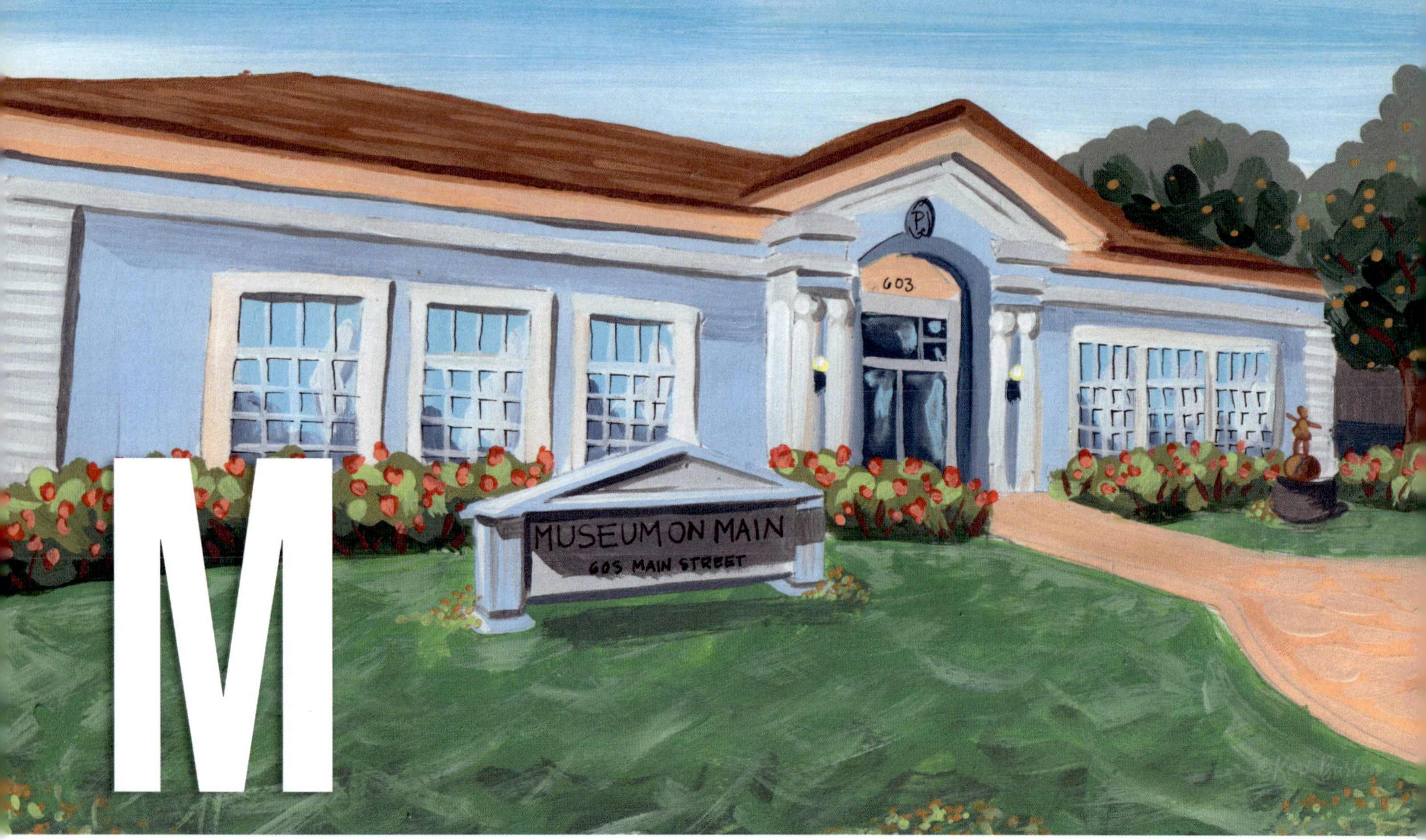

M

One of the most iconic buildings in the city is the downtown Museum on Main (MOM) located at Division Street and Main Street (pictured). The Women's Improvement Club donated this corner lot in 1912 to build a combined city hall and free public library to replace the old reading room (see letter L). Generous Phoebe Hearst (see letter E) donated furnishings to make the library a place that everyone wanted to visit and feel welcome. It is fitting that this carefully preserved building is now a local history museum that is open to the public, complete with an art gallery, fascinating artifacts, interactive exhibits, and a fun children's activity corner. Everyone at MOM works together to make history come alive through special events for kids and adults, walking tours, and open doors ready to greet you when you visit!

If you ever forget where you live, you'll be fine,
just proceed to downtown and look up at the sign.
If its dark, that's ok, cause I'm sure it will be on,
you can read it at night when the N stands for NEON!

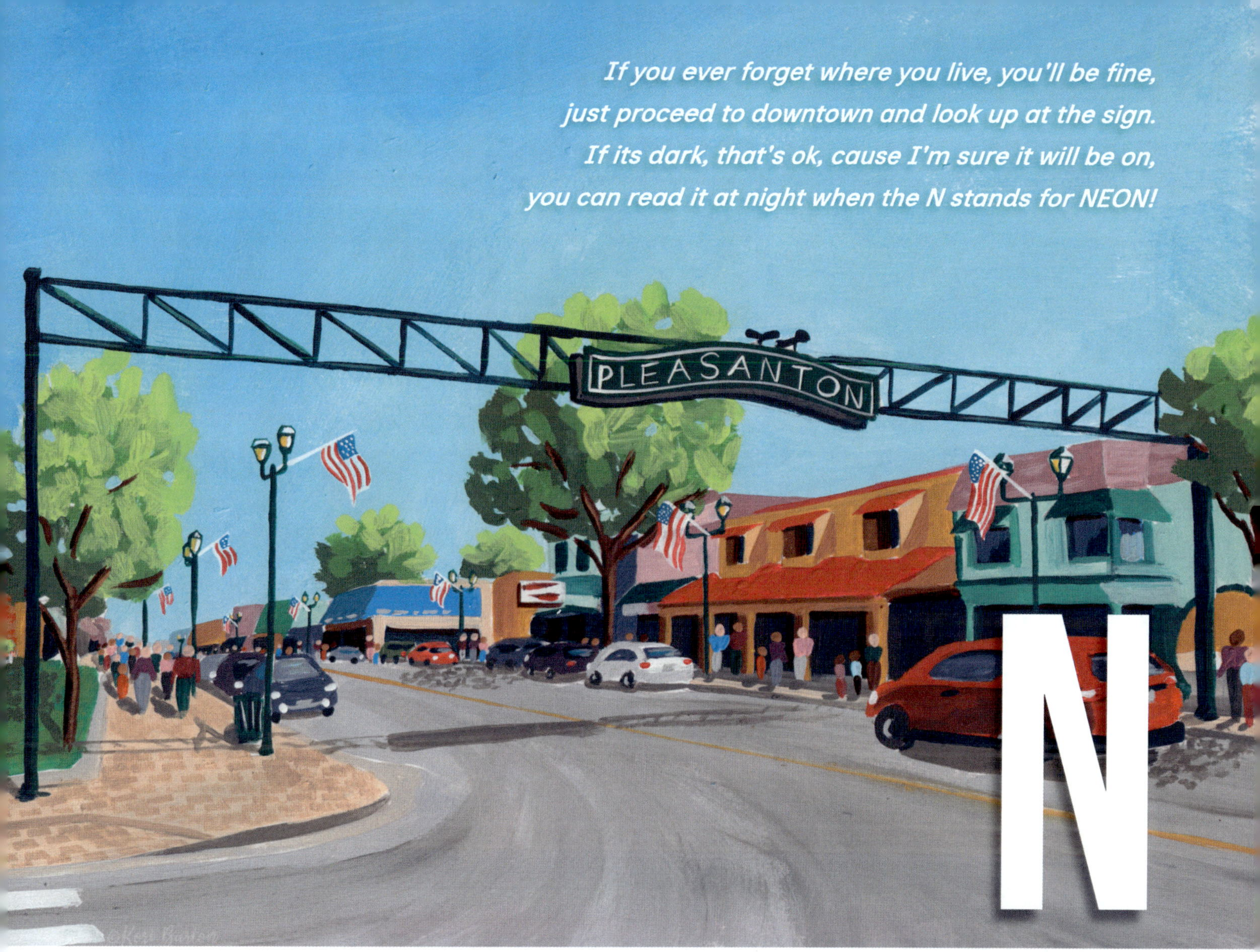

N

The iconic Pleasanton sign that spans Main Street (pictured) in front of the Museum on Main has greeted visitors and locals since 1932. Funded by the Women's Improvement Fund through raffles and socials, it was the first neon "electrified" sign in town. While it is now a lovely shade of Pleasanton Green, it was originally painted cobalt blue. And the sign is not just for looks; if you look closely at the top, you'll see an old siren and lights that were used for police and fire communication through the 20th century. If only this sign could talk, it would tell stories of the tens of thousands of people who have passed beneath its shadow (along with cattle, tractors, horses, and more!). After many decades, the sign needed refreshing, so it was carefully restored in 2005. As the sign approaches its 100th birthday, it is ready for another century of welcoming people to Pleasanton.

O stands for OPEN SPACE scattered about,
so you can get going, get moving, get out!
If fresh air, exercise, and great views are your goal,
you can hike all the way from Dublin to Sunol.

O

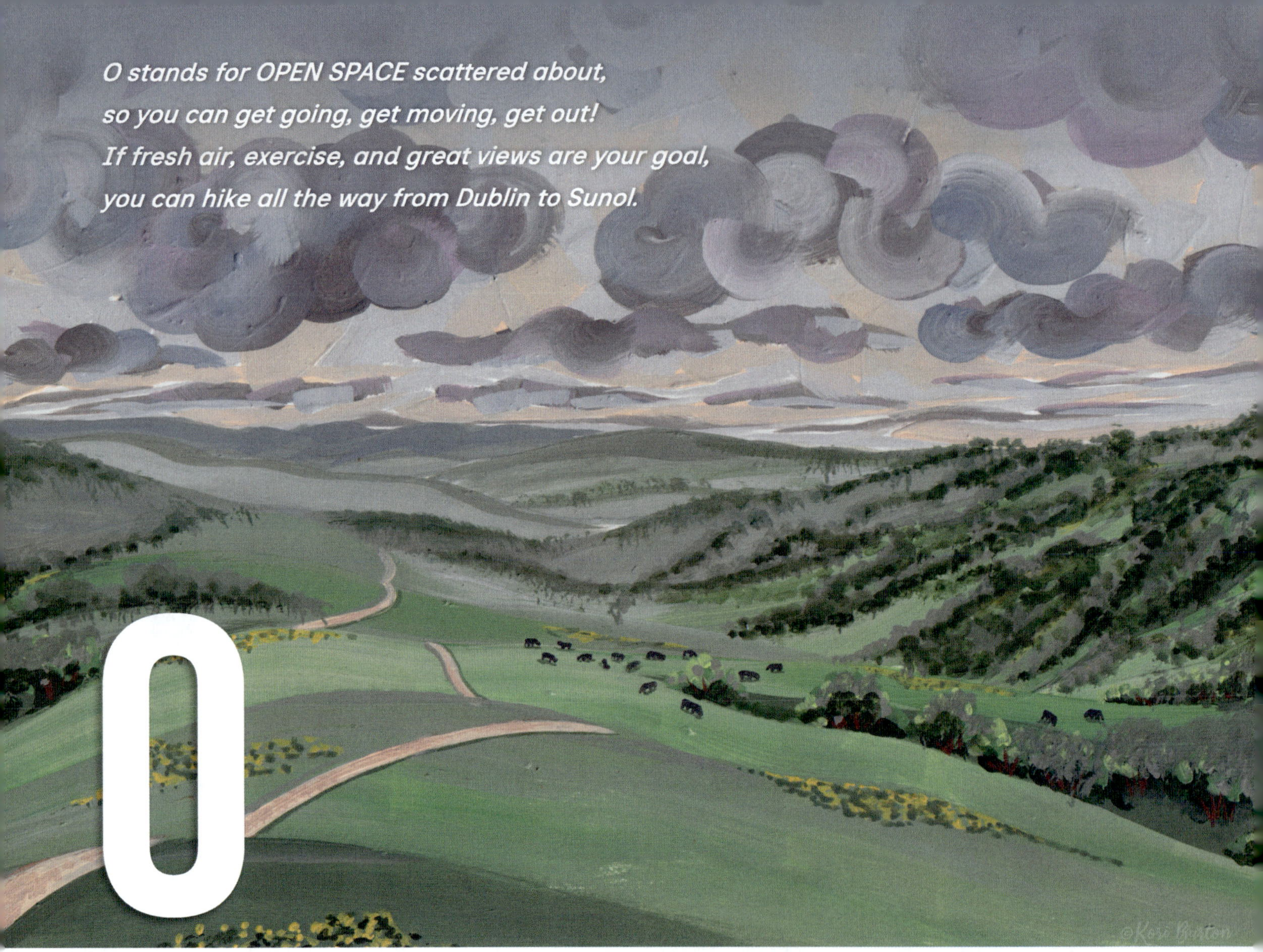

There is an abundance of wonderful opportunities for outdoor recreation in Pleasanton all year round. More than 60 miles of walking and biking trails wind through the city connecting people and places. With 46 community and neighborhood parks within the city's 24 square miles, you're never far from an outdoor place to play, read, walk, or bike. The beautiful Pleasanton Ridge Regional Park open space (pictured) along the city's western border provides a sprawling 9,090-acres of preserved land and dozens of trails that extend all the way to Sunol in the south. The diligent crew of park maintenance workers regularly inspect the city's trails and put a tremendous amount of time and effort into keeping the trails and parks clean, safe, and ready for everyone to enjoy. With dog parks, picnic areas, tennis courts, a community garden and a BMX park (see letter B), there is never an excuse to not enjoy the sunshine in Pleasanton!

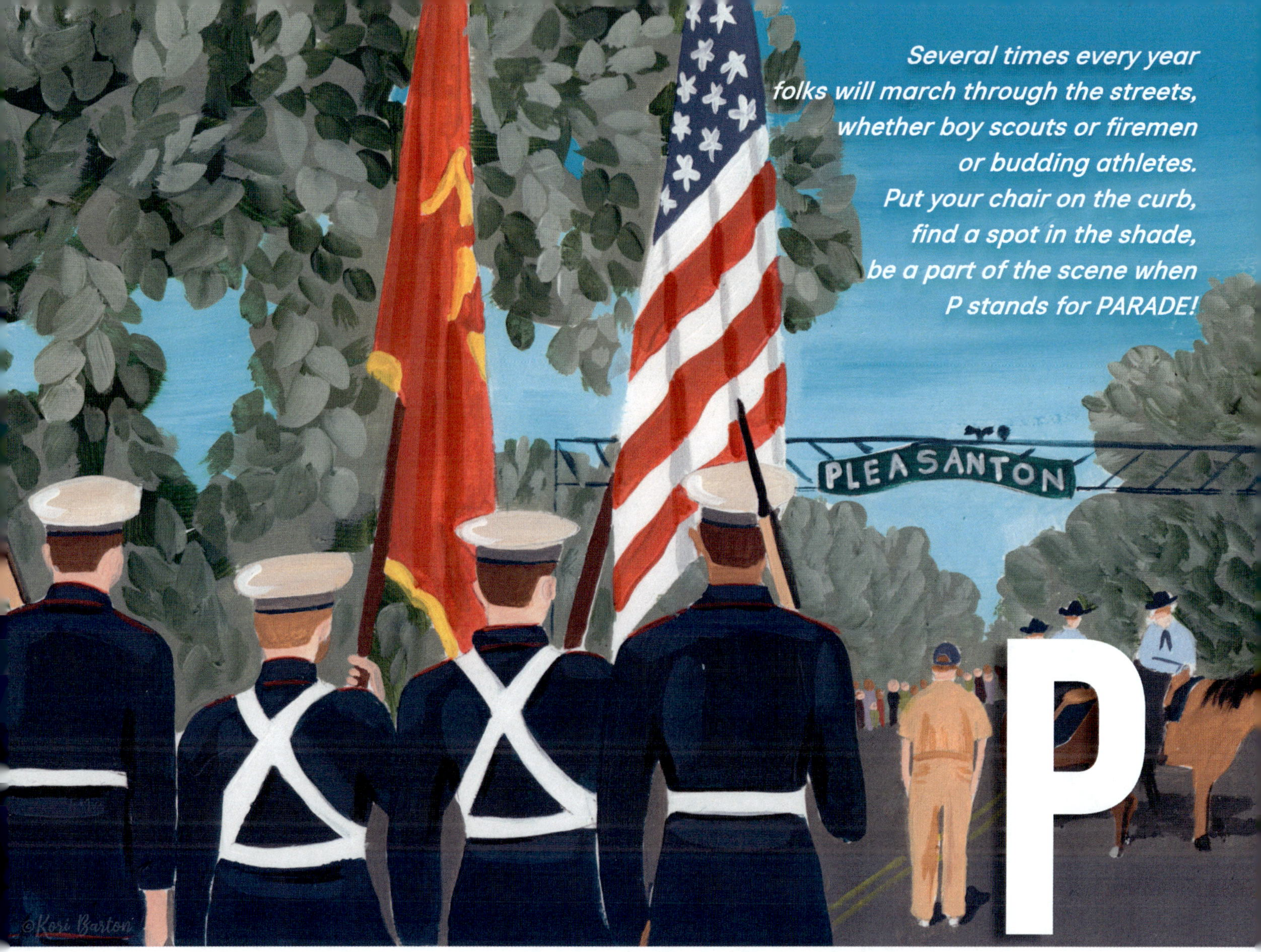

Several times every year
folks will march through the streets,
whether boy scouts or firemen
or budding athletes.
Put your chair on the curb,
find a spot in the shade,
be a part of the scene when
P stands for PARADE!

P

Main Street has never been a stranger to festive community parades. When the Alameda County Fair began in 1912, it included the first Alameda County Fair Parade. The parade marked the opening of the fair and drew large crowds to enjoy elaborate floats, vintage cars, marching bands, and local organizations. The Good Times Roll Parade, including the famously hilarious Balloon Platoon (visit the Museum on Main to learn all about it), began in 1974 and ran for a few years. They had special reunion parades 10 and 20 years later. The parade drew tens of thousands of spectators and traffic was backed up all the way to the freeway! The popular annual Hometown Holiday Parade in December is full of sparkling lights and the Veterans Day Parade (pictured) is held every November to honor our US military. How many Pleasanton parades have you attended?

Q stands for QUARRY where bulldozers dig
for rocks that will build things both little and big.
The sand might make concrete to build a nice a wall,
or a new office building fifteen stories tall!

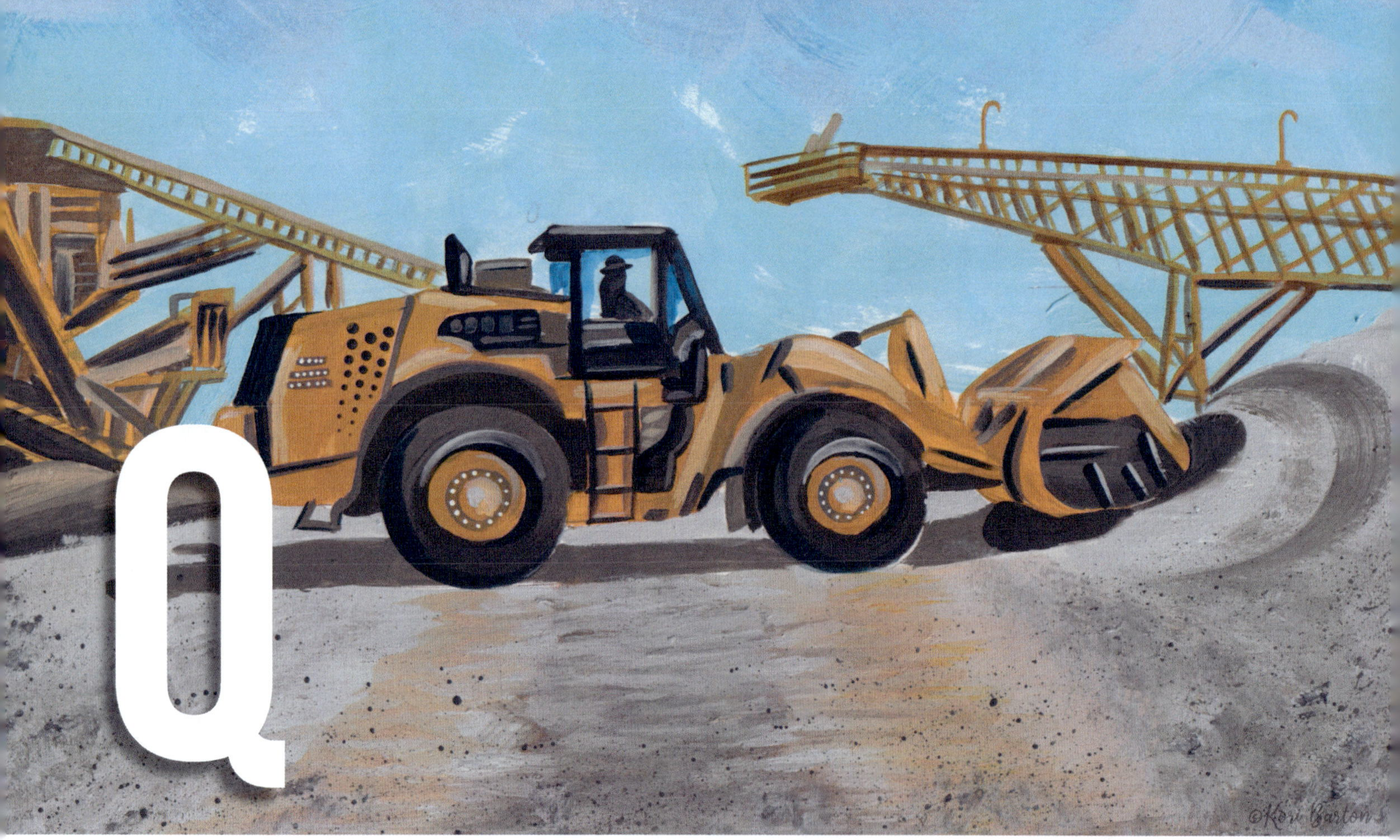

Q

Did you know that many of the homes, schools, parks, buildings, and roads in and around the Pleasanton area were built using materials from the aggregate quarries in Pleasanton? Including the paving of Stanley Boulevard! Since the early 1900s, the quarries spanning each side of Stanley Boulevard have been producing sand and gravel that are used in many different ways, such as in asphalt and concrete mixes. The quarries use a lot of machinery to make the job run smoothly, such as heavy-duty loaders (pictured) that scoop and move gravel and sand, and conveyor systems that quickly transport materials to stockpiles. The facilities have changed names and ownership quite a few times over the years, but they still produce building materials over a century later! Do you think your house is built in part by the Pleasanton quarries?

"What's that smell?" People ask as it wafts through their noses.
It begins with an R, could it maybe be ROSES?
At one time roses grew in this town by the mile,
bringing colors and smells to make everyone smile.

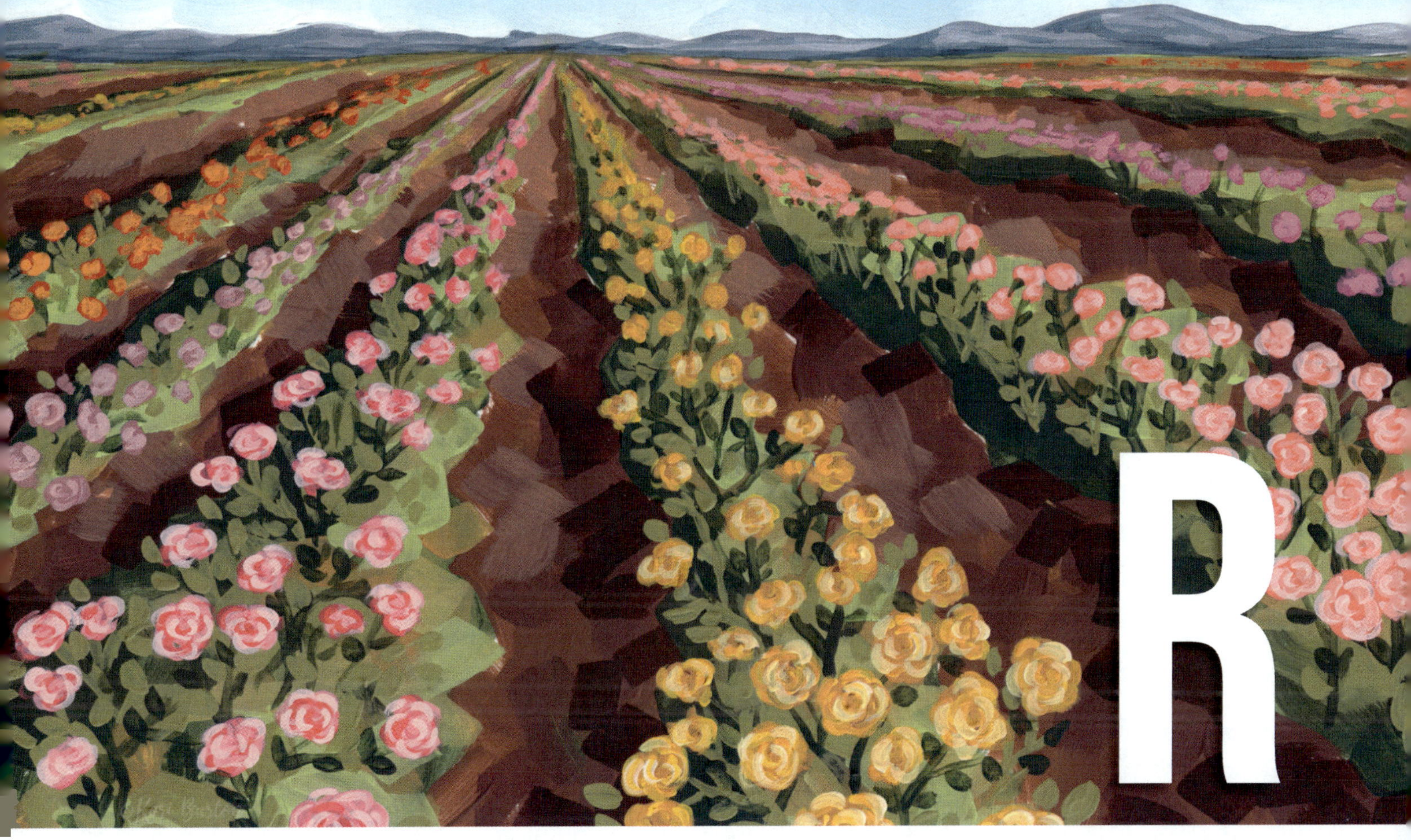

R

Can you imagine driving through Pleasanton and Livermore when 12 million rose plants were in bloom? Between 1938 through the 1960s, you would have seen thousands of rows of roses in every color growing throughout the region from late spring through early fall. The rose companies eventually had to relocate their operations, including the largest, Jackson and Perkins. Yet, because of Harry J. Harding, the roses left behind a colorful legacy. Community man and president of the First National Bank at 700 Main Street, Mr. Harding gave small rose bushes as appreciation gifts to his clients in 1935. His clients were so delighted that they brought beautiful rose blooms back to him in the years that followed. By 1938, the "thank you" roses became so numerous that they filled the entire bank lobby and an annual Mother's Day Rose Show was born! It's at a new location now at the Museum on Main, and you can visit the beloved Rose Show more than 85 years later.

SHADOW CLIFFS is a park, and it starts with an S.
Is there hiking and swimming? The answer is, yes!
And the fishing is good, if you care to partake,
at this former rock quarry turned into a lake.

S

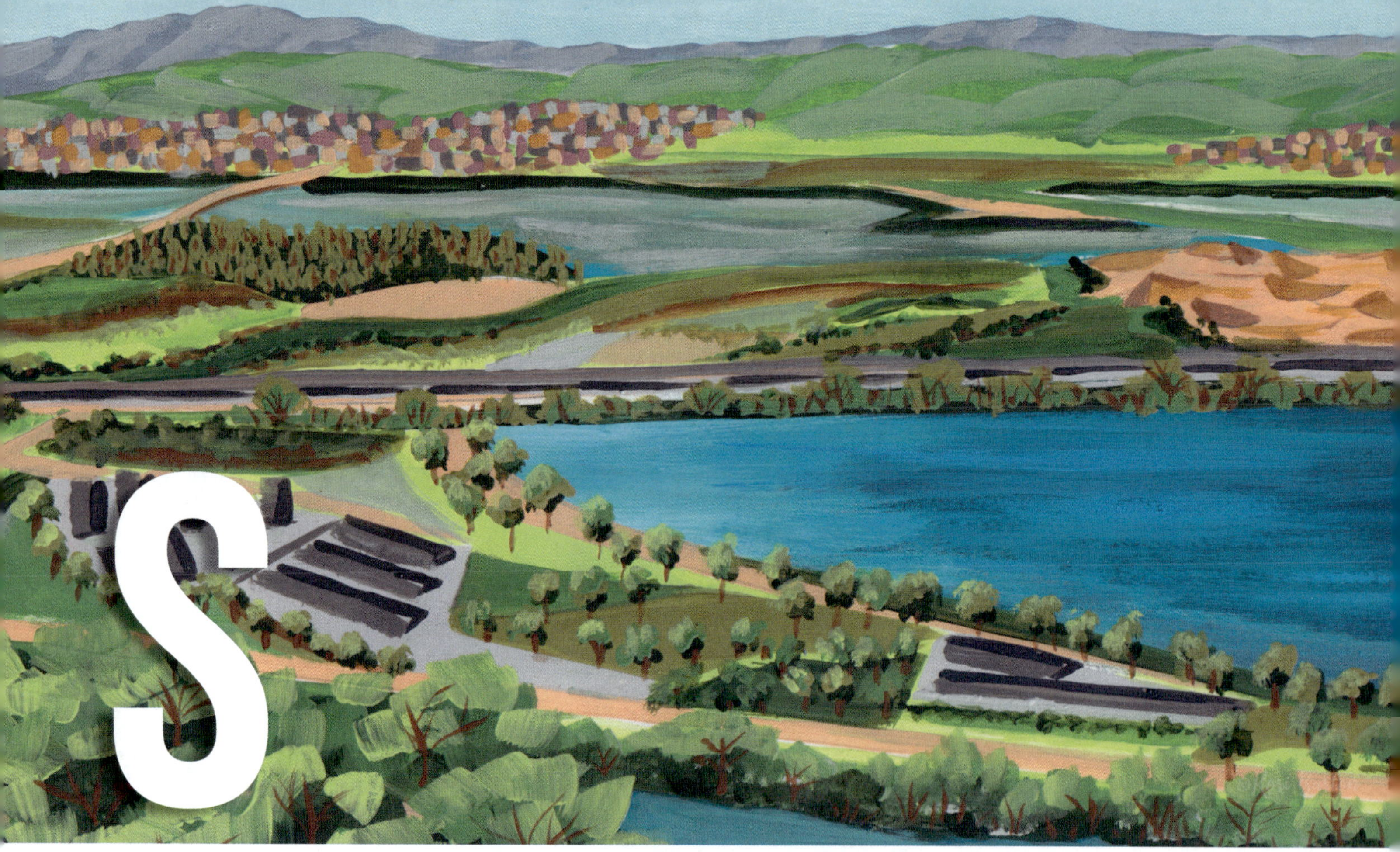

Henry J. Kaiser, a businessman, shipbuilder, health care provider, and industrialist who helped shape many aspects of the Bay Area, opened one of the quarries in Pleasanton in 1923 (see letter Q). When the aggregates at one of the dig sites were diminished, he donated the land to the East Bay Regional Park District (EBRPD). The former gravel quarry became Shadow Cliffs Regional Recreation Area in 1971. The park covers 266-acres and offers hiking trails, ponds, fishing, boating, picnic areas, and an 80-acre swimming lake. Of the 73 parks maintained by the EBRPD, Shadow Cliffs is one of the most popular swimming destinations in the area. Many locals may recall a set of blue water slides which were built into a hillside in the park in 1981. They were thoroughly enjoyed until they had to be removed in 2013 due to age and maintenance needs. If you like paddle boarding, bird watching, kayaking, or cooling off in summertime, visit Shadow Cliffs to enjoy all this and more.

T stands for THEATER, where now you watch plays,
but it was the firehouse in former days.
When old things are repurposed instead of destroyed,
the past is preserved and can still be enjoyed.

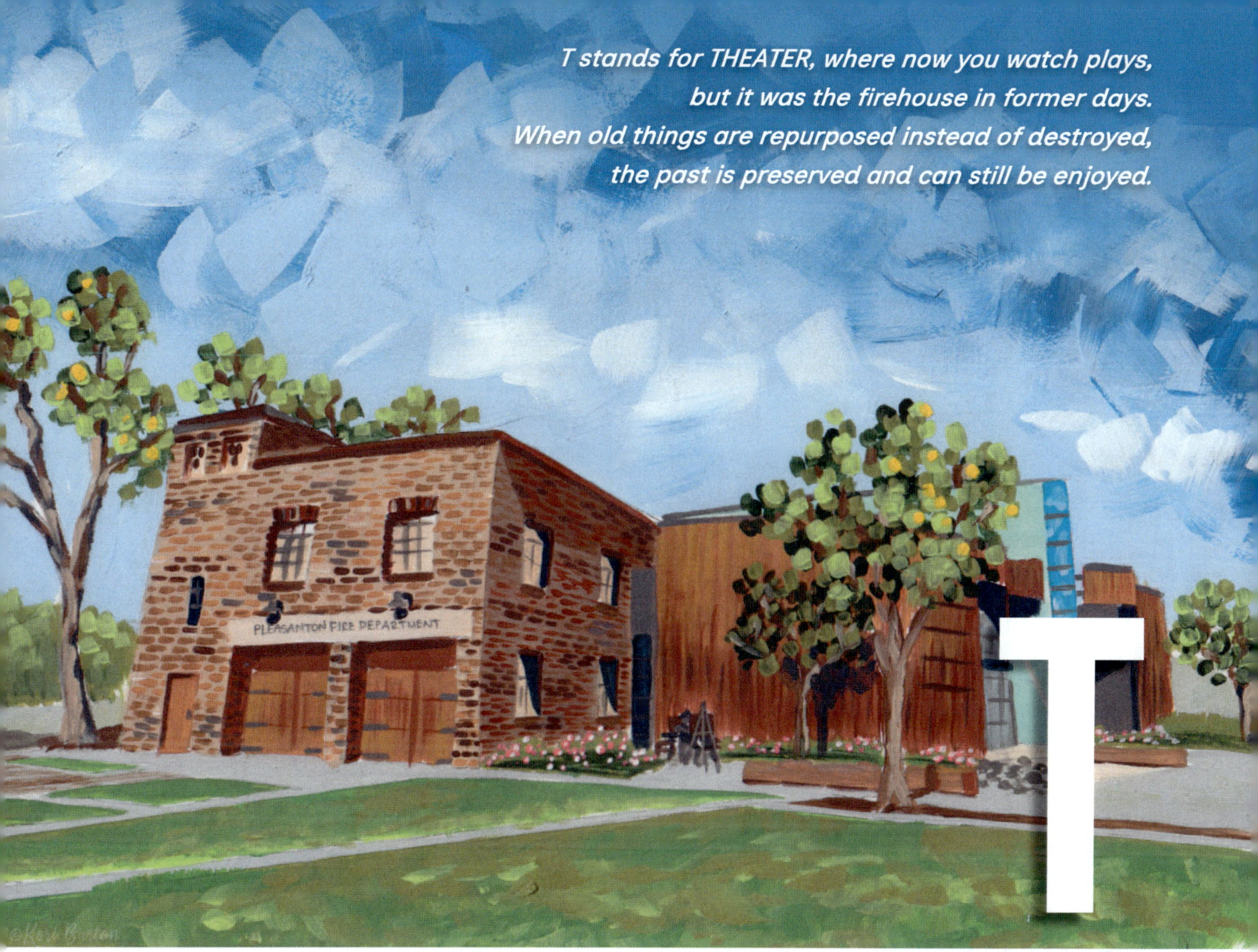

The Firehouse Arts Center in downtown Pleasanton is the ultimate fusion of new and old. In 1888, twenty local citizens began a volunteer fire department, which then became an official department 13 years later. A modest building was used to store the fire department's fire fighting equipment until 1927. A brick fire station (pictured) was built two years after to house fire engines and equipment. As more fire stations were built across the city, this old brick building was no longer needed, so it got a new lease on life as an arts center in 2010. Approximately 30,000 visitors now come to the Firehouse Arts Center each year to attend about 140 annual performances, various classes, camps, an art gallery, and much more! The thoughtful combination of preserved history, including many original artifacts and photos, along with modern arts and entertainment, makes this a true gem in the community.

When you study in school, learn to spell for Pete's sake,
'cause the name PleasAnton is a spelling mistake!
PleasOnton fought the war 'tween the Grey and the Blue,
and he fought for the UNION, which starts with a U.

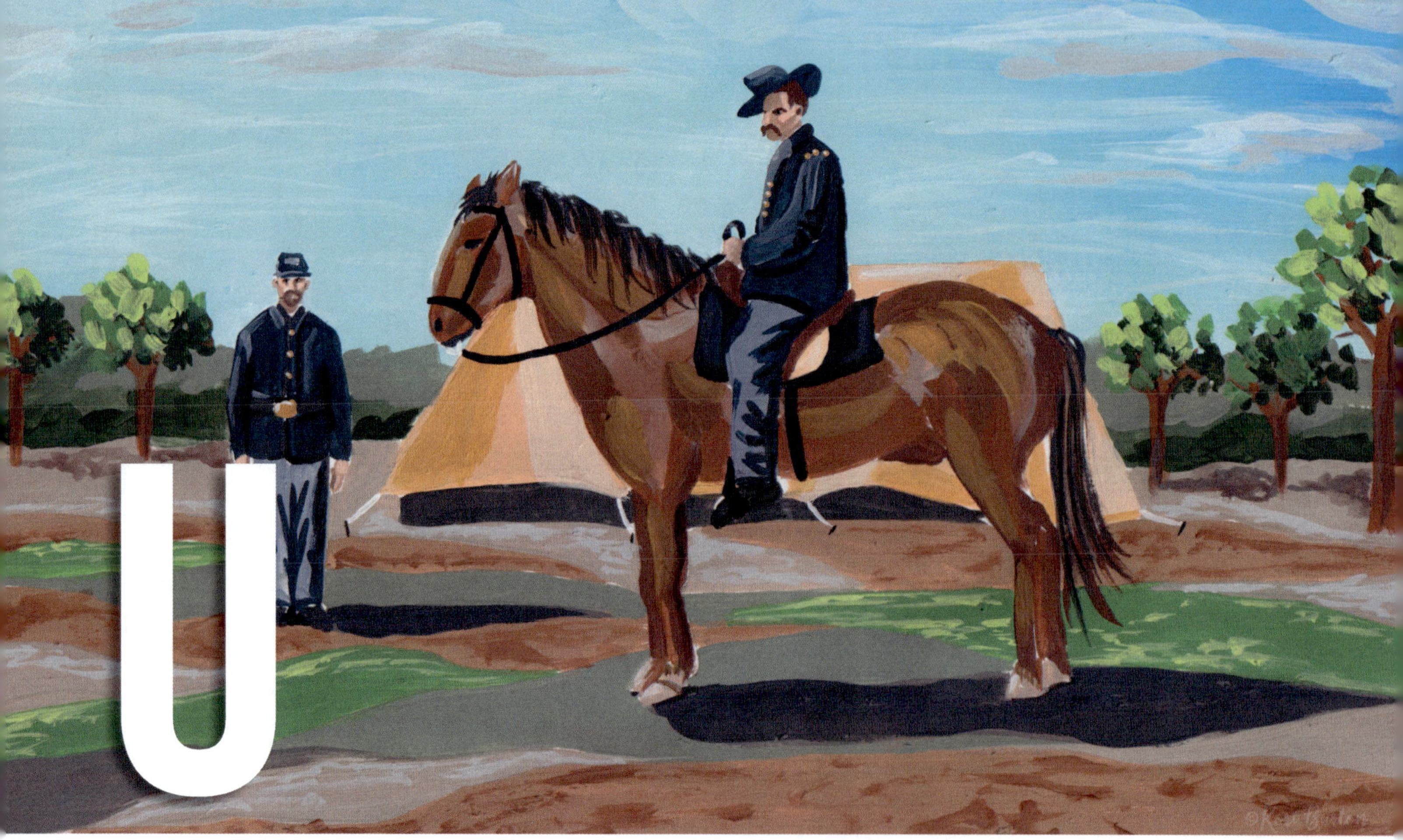

U

John Kottinger (see letter K) named this newly-established town "Pleasonton" in the 1860s in honor of Civil War Union Army Brevet Major General, Alfred Pleasonton (pictured). Ostensibly, because of a clerical typo in Washington D.C., the name of the city ended up being permanently misspelled with an "a" instead of an "o." General Pleasonton (1824-1897) served in the US Military from 1840 until he retired in 1868. He commanded the Calvary Corps during the Gettysburg Campaign, and led troops in the battles of Brandy Station, Antietam, Fredericksburg, and Chancellorsville, along with the battles of Bryam's Ford and Marais des Cygnes in Missouri. Our country also has his father, Stephen, to thank for heroically saving the original Declaration of Independence and the U.S. Constitution from a British invasion on Washington D.C. in 1814! General Pleasonton's grave is in Washington D.C.'s Congressional Cemetery, and his legacy lives on through Pleasanton being (mostly) named after him.

V stands for the VETERANS MEMORIAL HALL,
Where you can host a fundraiser,
wedding, or ball.
It honors brave vets
who were willing to perish,
defending the freedoms
we so deeply cherish.

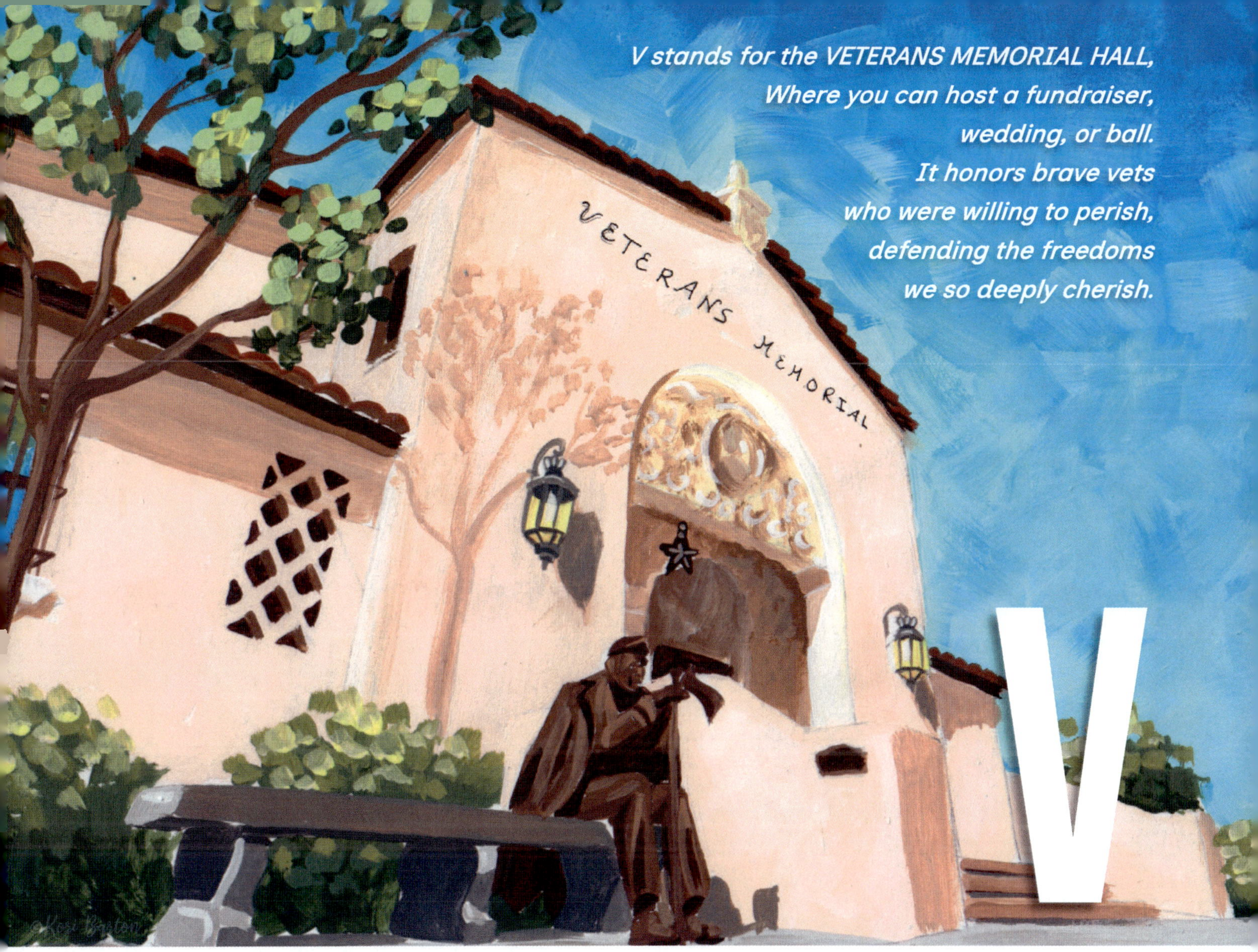

V

The iconic Veterans Memorial Building on Main Street was established in 1933 to honor all soldiers, sailors, and marines who served in the United States military during World War I. In 1941, the United Service Organization used this building to support the nearby military base Camp Parks established during World War II. It has also been a post for Veterans of Foreign Wars and the American Legion. Alameda County owned the building until the city of Pleasanton purchased it in 1997. Following many decades of use, updates were much needed to restore and preserve the historic building for the next generation. After seven long years of planning and restoration work, a public rededication ceremony was held on October 7, 2007 to celebrate the grand reopening. For nearly a century, this building has hosted countless events, meetings, dances, performances, parties, classes, and will host many more in years to come.

W for WAYSIDE PARK concerts in summers,
with musical genres to gladden all comers.
When blankets and chairs start to fill up the lawn,
you'd better act fast or your spot might be gone!

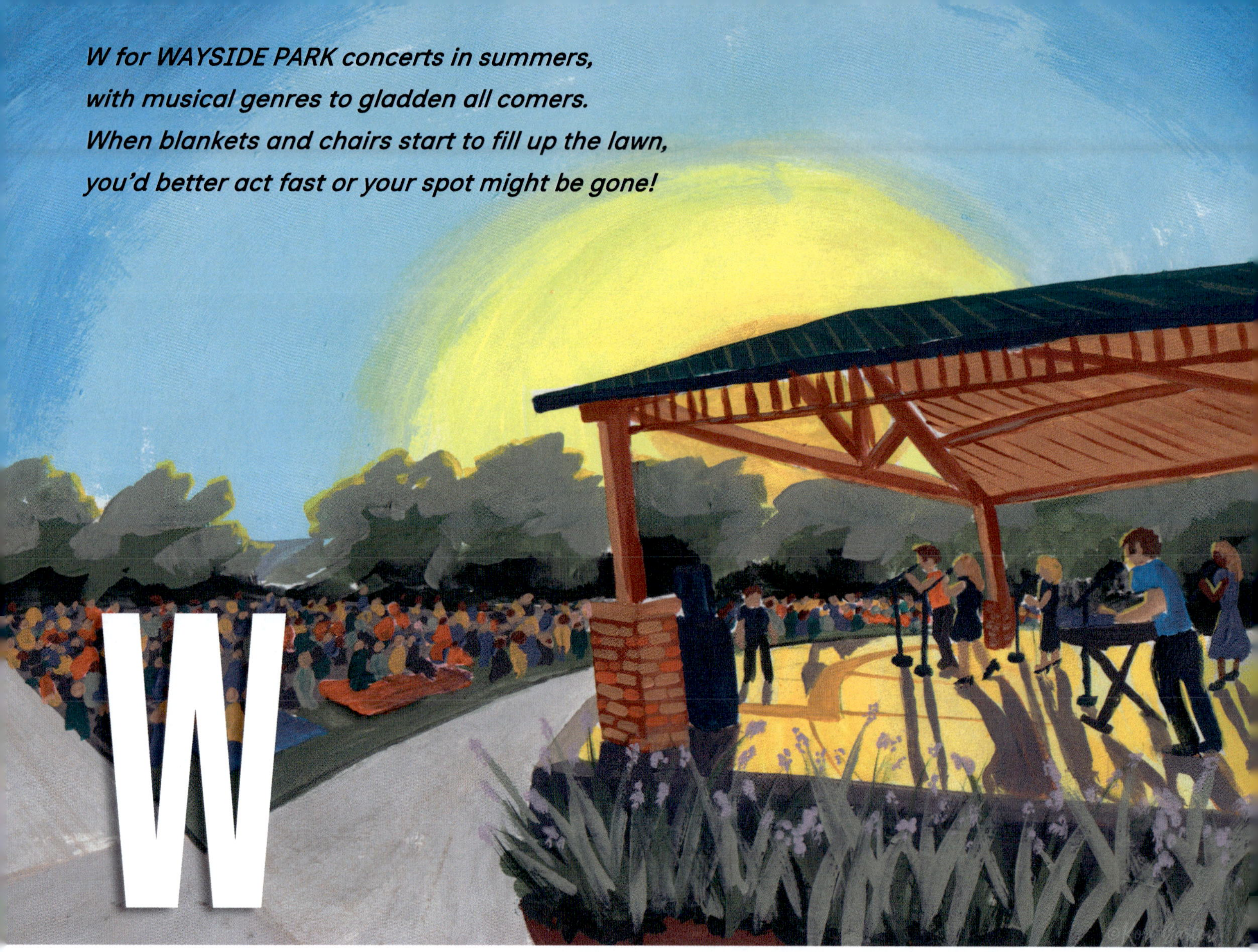

W

When summer rolls around, Lion's Wayside Park and Bandstand on First Street becomes an incredibly popular spot, especially on Friday nights. Concerts in the Park has been a treasured annual tradition for local families since it began in the 1980s. In recent years, nearly 2,000 people have attended concerts each week. Some especially eager concert goers often lay their picnic blankets down in the early morning to reserve their favorite space for the evening concert. A variety of musical genres are performed including country, rock, pop, dance, and reggae. A new and larger bandstand was built in June 2025 (pictured) complete with a dance floor in front of the stage for anyone who can't bear to revel in good music while sitting down.

X for railroad X-ING, the place where you stop
for a train to go by when you see the arms drop.
It might take a while for a mile-long freight,
but that's fine, because you get to watch while you wait!

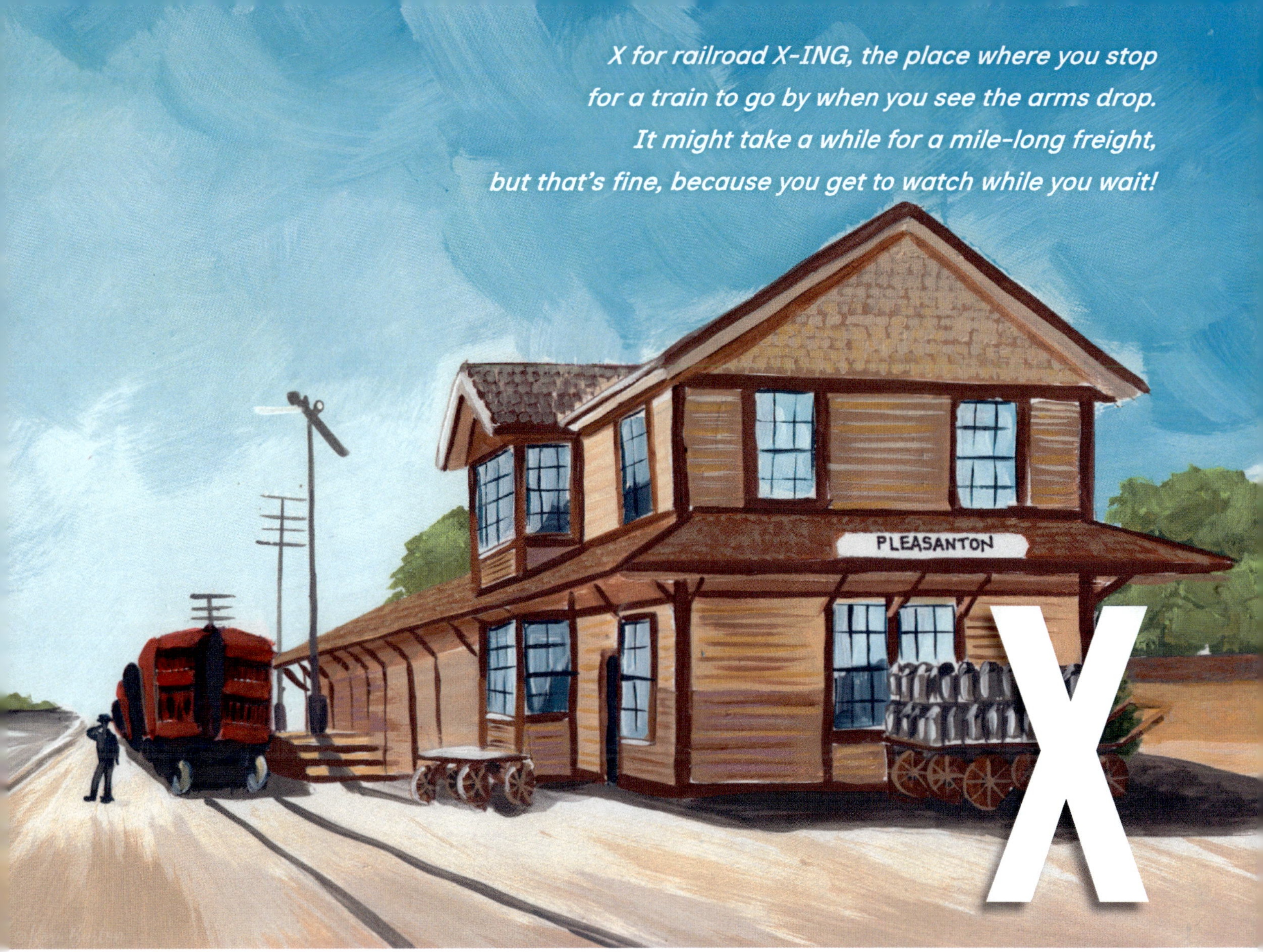

The railroad is an important part of commerce and connection in our country, and especially so in the 19th-century when roads were still very unreliable. When the first train rumbled through Pleasanton in September 1869, it marked the beginning of a bustling era of exporting copious amounts of produce and building products. The original train station (c. 1869) burnt down in a fire and was replaced by another one-story station, then a final two-story station around 1895 (pictured). The station has been re-purposed, but still stands on Neal Street. The railroad is owned by the Union Pacific Railroad (UP), formerly Southern Pacific, and you can still watch mile-long UP freight trains roll through town daily on their way to Oakland, Roseville and beyond. The purple and gray ACE commuter train, run by the San Joaquin Regional Rail Commission, began in 1998 and stops in Pleasanton many times daily. The ACE trains carry about 850,000 passengers each year to stations between Stockton and San Jose.

Y is for YEARLY FESTIVALS in town,
for more than a century, they've been the best 'round.
Classic cars, big parades, and markets galore,
they'll continue to host for 100 years and more!

Y

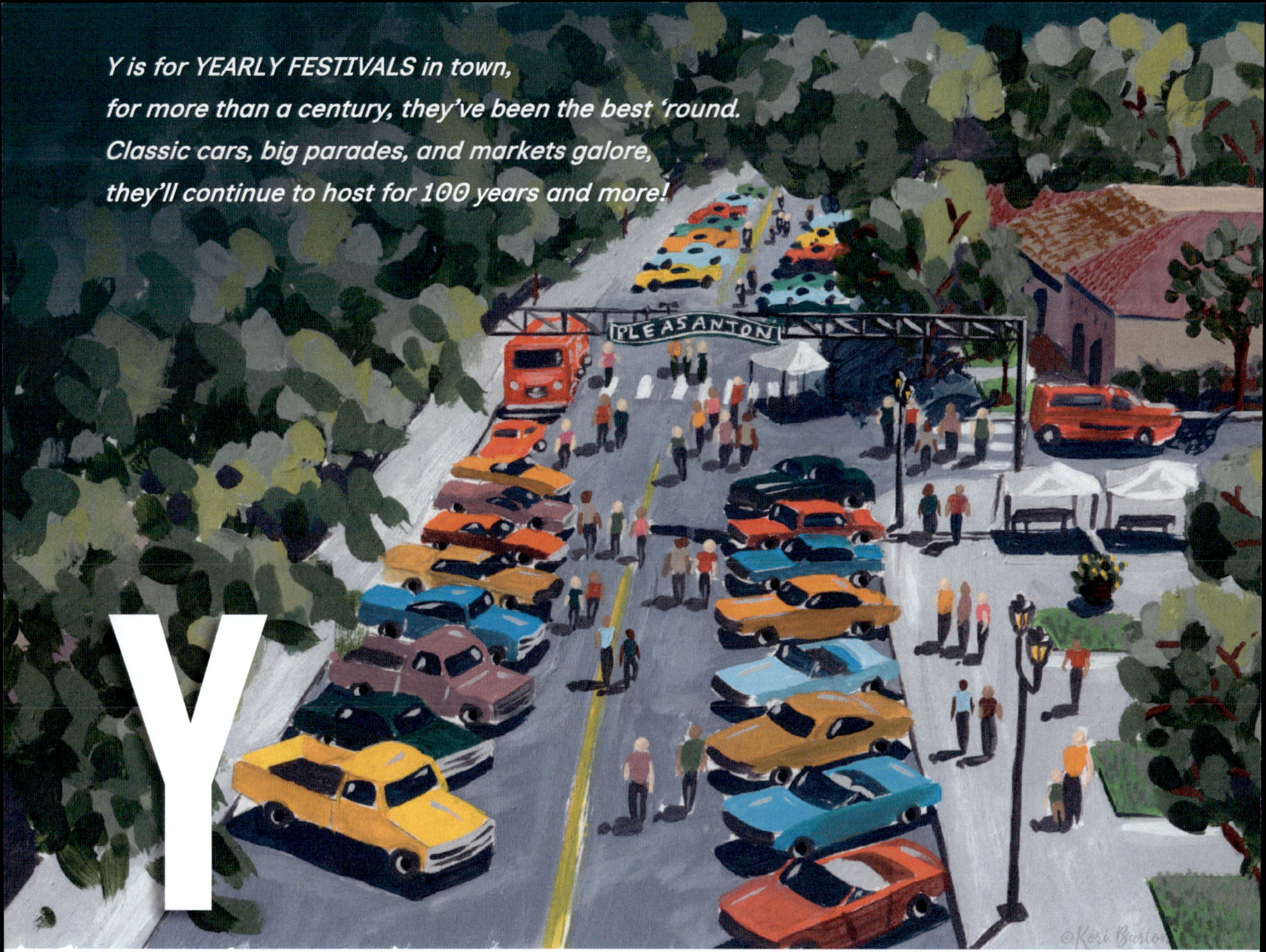

In addition to the delightful parades (see letter P) and summer concerts (see letter W), there are numerous family-friendly annual events in the city. The year-round Farmers' Market has filled the streets of downtown Pleasanton with colorful fruits, veggies, baked goods, meats, teas, and flowers on Saturday mornings since 1992. In summertime, more than 200 classic cars line Main Street for the popular Hot Rod Show (pictured). Couple those with Weekends on Main, events for St. Patrick's Day, Easter, Christmas, and Halloween, and you've got enough live bands, DJs, dancing, good food, and entertainment to last a whole year! Thanks to the continued effort of the Pleasanton Downtown Association, these fun happenings - and more! - are a big part of life for locals who look forward to the unforgettable events every year. Next time you see the Pleasanton Downtown Association booth at an event, stop by to say "Hi," and thank them for all their hard work to make the city a delightful and festive place to be.

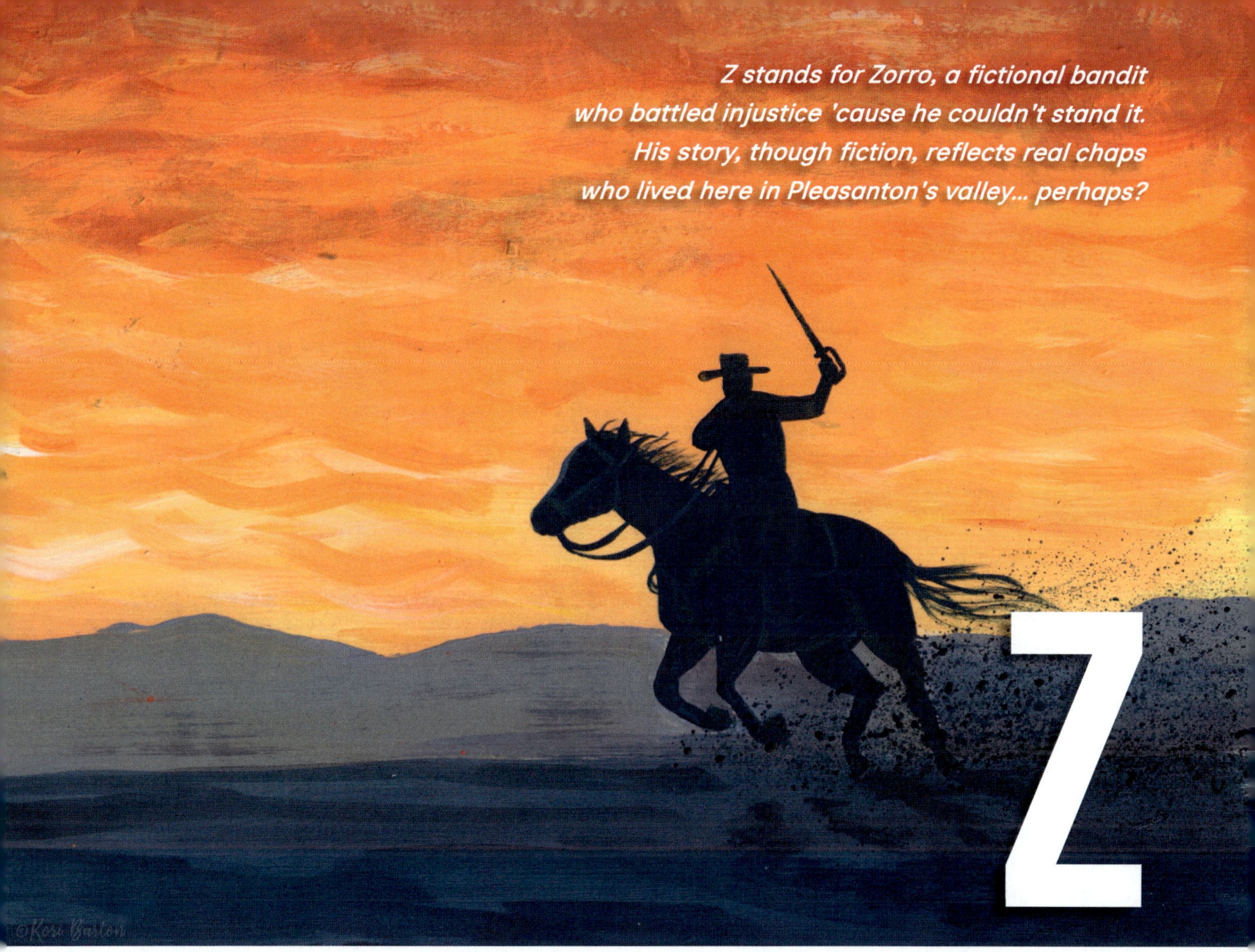

Z stands for Zorro, a fictional bandit
who battled injustice 'cause he couldn't stand it.
His story, though fiction, reflects real chaps
who lived here in Pleasanton's valley... perhaps?

Z

Back in the days of the Gold Rush, before Pleasanton got its current name, the region had a slightly different reputation. Alisal, as the Pleasanton area was known back then, was said to be a haunt for outlaws, including the mysterious Juaquin Murrieta. The legend of Murrieta is as sad as it is uncertain. The story goes that Murrietta was the victim of injustice after the Mexican-American War and became a kind of Robin Hood character as a result. He was feared by American gold miners across the state. A reward was offered for his capture, and California Rangers proclaimed that they had killed him in a gunfight in 1853. However, some who claimed to have known Murrieta and saw his body afterward said that the Rangers got the wrong man. Whether Murrieta was real figure or a legendary conglomeration of similar characters, and whether he actually met his end in that gunfight, the world may never know. But his legend lives on in characters like Zorro, and in the folklore of California towns like Pleasanton.

Location Information

Alviso Adobe Community Park
3465 Old Foothill Rd.

BMX Park
3320 Stanley Blvd.

Candy Cane Lane (December)
Walnut Dr.

Meadowlark Dairy
57 W. Neal St. I Meadowlarkdairy.com

Hacienda del Pozo de Verona, Phoebe Hearst Estate
707 Country Club Cir. (former site)

Alameda County Fair
2005 Valley Ave. I Alamedacountyfair.com

Pioneer Cemetery
5780 Sunol Blvd.

J.A. Bilz Wagon Factory
690 Main St. (former site)

Museum on Main
603 Main Street I Museumonmain.org

Kottinger Barn
200 Ray St.

Pleasanton Library
400 Old Bernal Ave. I Cityofpleasanton.gov

Neon Sign
Spanning Main Street (603 Main St.)

Pleasanton Ridge Regional Park
Foothill Rd.

Parades
Find info through the Pleasanton Downtown Association
pleasantondowntown.net

Aggregate Quarries
See them while driving down Stanley Blvd. toward Livermore.

Mother's Day Rose Show
Each May at the Museum on Main. Find info on the MOM website.

Shadow Cliffs Regional Recreation Area
2500 Stanley Blvd. I EBparks.org

The Firehouse Arts Center
4444 Railroad Ave. I Firehousearts.org

Veterans Memorial Building
301 Main St.

Lion's Wayside Park & Bandstand
4401 First St.

Find out about annual events online through the Pleasanton Downtown Association and the City of Pleasanton

Alphabet Check List

CHECK-OFF EACH FAMILY-FRIENDLY ACTIVITY AS YOU COMPLETE IT, AND THEN ADD YOUR OWN!

- [ ] Visit the Alviso Adobe Community Park
- [ ] Ride your bike at the BMX course
- [ ] Count the original wooden candy cane decorations on Candy Cane Lane in December
- [ ] Enjoy ice cream at the Meadowlark Dairy
- [ ] Find a local organization to support (volunteer, donate, etc.), just like generous Phoebe Hearst
- [ ] Discover old farming equipment in the American Farm Tractor Museum at the Alameda County Fairgrounds
- [ ] Quietly walk through the Pioneer Cemetery and find the headstones of the early pioneers
- [ ] Take a drive down Hopyard Road and imagine the street lined with towering, green hop plants
- [ ] Learn about buggy horse racing and jockeys at the Museum on Main
- [ ] Find the old hay hoist on the Kottinger Barn
- [ ] Borrow a local history book from the library
- [ ] Take a tour of the Museum on Main & art gallery
- [ ] Look for the old siren and lights atop the neon Pleasanton sign spanning Main Street
- [ ] Hike in the Pleasanton Ridge Regional Park
- [ ] Cheer from the sidelines for an upcoming parade (bonus points if you're IN the parade!)
- [ ] Drive past the quarries and watch the conveyor systems transport materials to stockpiles
- [ ] Attend the Mother's Day Rose Show in May
- [ ] Swim in the lake at Shadow Cliffs Regional Recreation Area
- [ ] Visit the art gallery at the Firehouse Arts Center
- [ ] Sit next to the bronze statue outside of the Veterans Memorial Building
- [ ] Dance at a summer concert at Wayside Park
- [ ] Count the cars on a passing Union Pacific freight train
- [ ] Attend a downtown event that you haven't been to before
- [ ] ____
- [ ] ____
- [ ] ____
- [ ] ____

Acknowledgements

We extend oodles of thanks to all members of the Museum on Main for your preservation of history, permission to use historical photos as painting references, and eagerness to share your time with us, especially Tony Cruz and Ken MacLennan. We appreciate you!

Without you, Cindy Hadden, this book would be riddled with typos and overused hyphens. Your eye for grammar, punctuation, and attention to detail makes all the difference. Thank you for the time and care you spent editing this book!

We made numerous wonderful connections with the community throughout this project. For your time, knowledge, and support, we are very grateful to each of you who helped shape this book. Thank you all! In no particular order: The City of Pleasanton (Communications Department, Public Works Department), Pleasanton Mayor Jack Balch, Alameda County Fairgrounds (Tiffany Lucian, Kayla Lueck and Steve Fedunak), Pleasanton Downtown Association (Gabrielle Welk and Mindy Louie), Beverly Lane, Meadowlark Dairy (Jesse Takens), Bill Vassar, Donna Dubose, Dozer, Robin Cruz, Pleasanton Weekly (Jeremy Walsh), Towne Center Books (Judy Wheeler), Vulcan Aggregates, Firehouse Arts Center, East Bay Regional Parks District, Anand Kumar Sankaran, ACE/San Joaquin Regional Rail Commission Public Relations Office, Union Pacific Public Affairs and Corporate Communications, Pleasanton Library staff, and our helpful children.

About the Authors

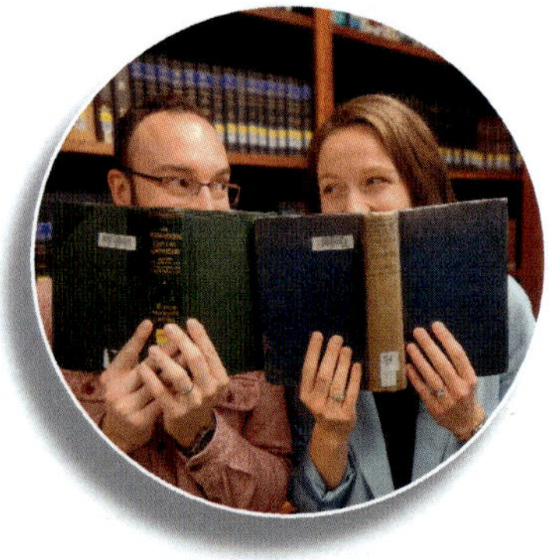

The Hometown Highlights Alphabet book series is written and illustrated by the happy husband-and-wife team, Sammy and Kori; homegrown Bay Area natives and fellow avid bookworms who share a particular affinity for the English language. They love to use their gifts of words and art to give thanks to God (1 Corinthians 10:31). You'll find them with their kids biking on local trails, hiking in the open spaces, and playing ball at community parks.

If you would like to say "Hi" or learn about upcoming book releases in the Hometown Highlights Alphabet Series, please visit: www.HometownAlphabet.com

Selected References

Alfred Pleasonton (n.d.). American Battlefield Trust. Accessed from: https://www.battlefields.org/learn/biographies/alfred-pleasontonst

Alfred Pleasonton (n.d.). Find a Grave. Accessed from: https://www.findagrave.com/memorial/12945/alfred-pleasonton

Art, Culture, and History (n.d.). Accessed from: https://visittrivalley.com/blog/the-history-behind-the-alameda-county-fairgrounds-horse-race-track/

Bay Area News Group (March 17, 2005). When the Good Times Rolled in Pleasanton. Accessed from: https://www.eastbaytimes.com/2005/03/17/when-the-good-times-rolled-in-pleasanton/

Bregel, Brandi (December 17, 2025). The Birthplace of Horse Racing in California: Pleasanton, CA. Accessed from: https://www.fastandfuriouspleasanton.com/where-is-the-pleasanton-ca-racing-competition-held

Campos Rajs, Elizabeth (October 5, 2007). A Place for Veterans. Accessed from: https://www.pleasantonweekly.com/cover-story/2007/10/05/a-place-for-veterans/

Falmouth, Va. Capt. George A. Custer and Gen. Alfred Pleasonton on horseback (n.d.). Accessed from: https://www.loc.gov/pictures/item/2018666289/resource/

Grossman, Deborah (May 8, 2025). Pleasanton Farmers' Market At Its Peak. Accessed from: https://www.pleasantonweekly.com/cover-story/2025/05/08/pleasanton-farmers-market-at-its-peak/

Jetter, Cathy (February 25, 2005). Long Live Our Landmark. Accessed from: https://www.pleasantonweekly.com/morgue/2005/2005_02_25.arch25.shtml

Johnson, Autumn (June 14, 2013). Saying Goodbye to the Shadow Cliffs Waterslides. Accessed from: https://patch.com/california/pleasanton/saying-goodbye-to-the-shadow-cliffs-water-slides

Klimczak, Nicole (July 9, 2016). Joaquin Murietta - The Man Whose Life Provided Inspiration for Zorro. Accessed from: https://www.ancient-origins.net/history-famous-people/joaquin-murrieta-man-whose-life-provided-inspiration-zorro-006257

Lane, Bob and Pat (1988). The Amador-Livermore Valley

Lofft, Patrick M. *Wander a Timeline from 2008 A.D. Back to 3240 B.C.* (February 2009). Accessed from: https://d3n8a8pro7vhmx.cloudfront.net/cchs/pages/566/attachments/original/1469657742/Alviso_Articles.pdf?1469657742

May, Melissa (2021). Newspaper Unknown. 'Candy Cane Lane' Readies for Holidays.

Mrs. Phoebe Hearst Dies at Her Home in Pleasanton (April 19, 1919). Sausalito News. Accessed from: https://cdnc.ucr.edu/?a=d&d=SN19190419.2.14&e=-------en--20--1--txt-txIN--------

Patent, Plow (1886). Accessed from: https://patentimages.storage.googleapis.com/29/2f/47/911447aaafc29a/US351154.pdf

Patent, Two-Wheeled Buggy (1892). Accessed from: https://patentimages.storage.googleapis.com/aa/bd/38/d72e57a3ea66fe/US475974.pdf

Patent, Two-Wheeled Vehicle (1882). Accessed from: https://patents.google.com/patent/US262273A/en

Pleasanton Downtown Historic Context Statement (March 2015). Accessed from: https://www.cityofpleasantonca.gov/assets/our-government/community-development/handouts/downtown-historic-context-statement.pdf

Pleasanton Public Library: A Brief History (n.d.). Accessed from: https://www.friendsofthepleasantonlibrary.org/assets/pdf/Pleasanton_Public_Library_History.pdf

Pleasanton Ridge Regional Park (n.d.). East Bay Parks. Accessed from: https://www.ebparks.org/parks/pleasanton-ridge
The Evoloution of Motocross (November 5, 2025). Accessed from: https://enginestories.com/moto/from-scramble-to-supercross-traces-of-the-rich-and-interesting-history-of-motocross/

Trujano, Christian (July 1, 2025). Pleasanton Celebrates Reopening of Lions Wayside Park After Renovations. Accessed from: https://www.pleasantonweekly.com/pleasanton/2025/07/01/pleasanton-celebrates-reopening-of-lions-wayside-park-after-renovations/

Wainright, Mary-Jo, Museum on Main. *Images of America Pleasanton* (2007).

Walsh, Jeremy (April 8, 2026). Pleasanton Rose Show Moves to Museum on Main for 86th Installment. Accessed from: https://www.pleasantonweekly.com/family-lifestyle/2026/04/08/pleasanton-rose-show-moves-to-museum-on-main-for-86th-installment/

What BMX taught a generation: a ride from Southern California dirt to global podiums (March 2026). Accessed from: https://worldofbmx.com/bmx/what-bmx-taught-a-generation-a-ride-from-southern-california-dirt-to-global-podiums.html

Willard, Ruth Hendricks (1988). Alameda County, California Crossroads.

Made in the USA
Coppell, TX
21 June 2026

82219813R00021